Art Rockwood's
NEWFOUNDLAND & LABRADOR
Trivia
The Sequel

Harry Cuff Publications Limited
St. John's · 1994

Appreciation is expressed to the Canada Council for publication assistance.

The publisher acknowledges the financial contribution of the Cultural Affairs Division of the Department of Tourism and Cultural Affairs, Government of Newfoundland and Labrador, which has helped make this book possible.

Canadian Cataloguing in Publication Data

Rockwood, Art, 1946-

Art Rockwood's Newfoundland and Labrador Trivia : the sequel

ISBN 0-921191-95-2

1. Newfoundland -- Miscellanea. I. Title. II. Title: Newfoundland and Labrador trivia : the sequel.

FC2161.6.R633 1994   971.8'002   C94-950275-8
F1122.5.R633 1994

Cover photos: Manfred Buchheit

Printed by

Published by
Harry Cuff Publications Ltd.
94 LeMarchant Road
St. John's, Newfoundland
A1C 2H2

Trivia . . .

. . . the sequel

to Michael F. Harrington
and
to the memory of J.R. Smallwood
Two Barrelmen, who devoted their lives to
''making Newfoundland better known to Newfoundlanders''.

Contents

Introduction

As soon as the *Newfoundland and Labrador Trivia* book hit the shelves people started asking "Will there be a volume two?". I knew in the back of my mind that there could be because there had been lots of new bits and pieces filed away before *Newfoundland and Labrador Trivia* was finished. I had several items which I didn't have time to check out fully, and there were new pieces being offered all the time. The morning after the book went on sale in St. John's I received a call at home from a man who had just heard my interview with Ray Bellew on CBC's "Weekend AM" program, during which I had said "who knows, maybe there will be a volume two". The caller said "I've got a great piece of information for you if you decide to do a new book". And this was the way it went. People would constantly give me tidbits of information they thought good enough for inclusion in a second volume, should there be one. In fact, during our interview Ray Bellew gave me one of the juiciest pieces of Newfoundland and Labrador trivia I had ever come across.

So I gathered all the information I could and, as I had done with volume one, began my search for verification. Again there are many who gave assistance in one way or another to the venture, and to whom I owe my thanks — first of all, to Liz Stanford of Inter Library Loans at MUN, without whose help I'd probably still be working on chapter one of the first book. Also I would like to note the contributions of Philip Hiscock and Peter Narvaez at MUN Folklore, Heather Wareham at MUN's Maritime History Archives, Hans Rollmann of MUN's Religious Studies Faculty, Ed Pike, Gary Hebbard, Ray Bellew, John O'Mara, Paul Vincent, Bob Lewis, Albert Colbourne, Dr. Noel Murphy, Paul Kenney, Frank Bartlett, Frank Rowe, Frank Galgay, Roland Burke, Dave Harlan, and also my computer research partners: Veronica, Archie, Jughead, Gopher and 'The Web'. They made some of the digging easy.

And as always I owe a real vote of thanks to the Trivia Show listeners and callers. As they read through this volume, a lot of those people will probably notice some little tidbit that they contributed.

Corrections

Ah well, it's time to hang my head in shame. As the old saying goes, "Nobody's perfect". Anyone who writes a book that deals in facts, facts, and more facts can expect to miss something. And yes, there were a couple of mistakes in the first Trivia book. (Which I suppose isn't too bad considering the amount of information I had to deal with.) I decided when I wrote the *Newfoundland and Labrador Trivia* book that if mistakes were pointed out to me, I'd do my best to admit my mistakes in print and I asked if people had suggestions, comments or corrections that they contact me. And several people did. Thankfully, most reactions were compliments, but people weren't at all shy about pointing out where I went wrong either. Certainly, I didn't mind this one bit — it kept me on my toes. But, three of the mistakes were simply ones where *I knew* the difference, I had just read the material over and over so many times that it just passed above my head:

1.) Dr. Frederick Grant Banting was killed near Musgrave *Harbour*, not Musgrave*town*. The mistake that has been pointed out to me more often than any other. How this one ever zipped by me I don't know. Just before writing that section I had visited the park in Musgrave Harbour where the remaining wreckage of Banting's aircraft is resting.

2.) The next embarrassing mistake concerned Newfoundland-born Egyptologist Samuel Mercer. Samuel *Alfred Browne* Mercer to be exact, and not Samuel Arthur Brown Mercer. I caught this one just a little too late. The book had already gone to press.

3.) In the referring to one Father O'Brien of Bay Bulls who invented a method of deflecting torpedoes, I spoke of World War II and Prime Minister Edward Morris (who incidentally was created Baron Morris in 1918 and became only the second Newfoundlander to sit in the British House of Lords — any guesses as to whom was the first?). As one reader pointed out, the chronology was a little off. Edward Patrick Morris was the Prime Minister during the Great War, usually known to us as World War I. Again a fact I knew, but for some reason I had put down World War II by mistake.

Finally, one of those cases of not digging quite far enough. This would be fine, except that I said in my original introduction that in order to be as accurate as possible, I dug to the best of my ability. In one case I should have gone just a bit deeper. In the Music section, I wrote about Newfoundlander Brian MacLeod who had been a rock musician with the popular group Chilliwack. I mentioned that Brian was the son of Bob MacLeod, a musician and announcer with CBC (and, before that, BCN). I had seen that information written down somewhere and had spoken to a couple of people who knew Brian who said that he was Bob's son. Just after the book came out I received a call from Corner Brook. It was Bob MacLeod Jr. He said "Art, I liked the book, but I want to correct one thing. I didn't have a brother Brian, in fact I don't have any brother at all." Bob Jr. is a dentist in Corner Brook who did follow in his father's musical footsteps. In fact, one of his accomplishments is something of a trivia item in itself: on November 6, 1993 he played every hymn in the Anglican Hymn Book, about 800 in all, in about seven hours. He started playing at 8:30 in the morning and finished at 3:30 in the afternoon, raising money for the St. John the Evangelist Cathedral Development Fund. (How's that for trivia, Bob?)

As with the last book, I once again ask that anyone who finds a mistake in the information please let me know. In fact I enjoy fielding any and all comments — whether compliments, criticisms or suggestions.

More Notable Newfoundlanders

This is a continuation of one of the most popular sections of *Newfoundland and Labrador Trivia*. A lot of people commented on how much they enjoyed that particular part of the book; how they didn't know that so many Newfoundlanders had become famous elsewhere. And we've barely scratched the surface. The more I dug the more I found.

Clarence Wiseman

Clarence Wiseman was born in 1907, while his parents were officers at the Moreton's Harbour corps of the Salvation Army. Most records list his birthplace as Moreton's Harbour, but there are those in the area who maintain that he was actually born in nearby Whales Gulch (since renamed Valley Pond), where the majority of the corps congregation lived. Wiseman could trace his family's history on the Island back to 1720 and the family name is still a common one in Trinity Bay and western Notre Dame Bay. While still a boy his parents were transferred to the Canadian mainland. In 1927 Clarence Wiseman was commissioned an officer in the Salvation Army. Then he started to move up through the ranks and became chaplain for the Canadian Army during World War II. In 1945 he moved back to Newfoundland where he became territorial commander of the Salvation Army, a position he held until 1957. Then it was on to become chief secretary for all of Canada, then to Africa and then London before becoming territorial commander for Canada and Bermuda. In 1974 he became the worldwide commander for the denomination, a position he held until 1977. General Wiseman died in 1985.

Peter F. Windsor

There is a small town about 30 miles from Kimberley, South Africa called Windsorton. The town is named after Peter F. Windsor who moved to South Africa from Aquaforte. He went into the diamond mining business where he made his fortune, for a time serving as mayor of Kimberley.

Jim Dempsey

During the early days of World War II, probably the most feared of the German vessels in the North Atlantic was the battleship *Bismarck*. This warship and her crew were responsible for the loss of numerous Allied vessels. On May 18, 1941, she sank the British ship *Hood*. Attempts to track the Bismarck proved futile. She would avoid searchers every time. But in late May, 1941, two wireless operators, one in Newfoundland and another in Bermuda, picked up the radio signal from the *Bismarck* as she broadcast back to Germany. The Canadian Navy had set up a direction-finding station in Gander and every morning the operator on duty would be given a list of frequencies to monitor, and times to listen in. The operators didn't know which ships they were taking bearings on, all they knew was that they were monitoring German vessels: battleships, destroyers and U-Boats.

The *Bismarck* was finally sunk by the British Navy on May 27, 1941. A couple of days after the sinking Jim Dempsey was called in by the communications officer in Gander. The officer told him "You got the best bearing you'll ever take". He wasn't too forthcoming with information but Jim Dempsey realized it was something important. He went back through the logbooks and found his answer. Dempsey and a Bermuda operator had plotted the location of the *Bismarck*. Further investigation revealed that the coordinates Dempsey had noted in his logbook were accurate within 30 miles.

Jim Dempsey never received any commendation for what he had done, and unfortunately the logbooks were destroyed. The Royal Air Force, being meticulous about military secrecy, took all the materials from the direction-finding station to the dump. Dempsey said he watched as they loaded the old logbooks onto a truck. He said he was tempted to remove the one with the *Bismarck* finding in it, but his honesty and sense of duty prevailed.

John (Jack) Ford

Jack Ford was the only Newfoundlander to have survived an atomic bomb blast. He was living in Port aux Basques when the War broke out, enlisted in the Royal Artillery and transferred to the Royal Air Force when he arrived in England in 1940. After training he was sent to Singapore. In early 1942, Ford was captured by the Japanese at Caroet in Java, and on December 7, 1942, was transferred to the Nagasaki Prisoner of war camp — Fukuoka Number 2. Ford and his fellow prisoners, mostly British and American, received two meals per day, and for the next three and a half years had to endure the hardships imposed on them by the captors. The prison camp was located on an island in Nagasaki Harbour, where there was a shipyard in which Ford was forced to work. On August 9, 1945, he was working at the shipyard cutting steel. He'd left to go get a jug of water when the bomb hit. Ford was knocked to the ground unconscious. Wood and glass flew through the air and a sheet of steel dropped nearby. A few minutes later he came to. People were screaming around him, the heat was intense and he could see fire in all directions. Above him a huge mushroom cloud rose into the sky. The bomb had struck only a mile away, but miraculously Ford was unhurt. Although 75,000 people had been killed in the city of Nagasaki, no one on the island had died as a result of the blast. Ford found shelter and waited for the all-clear signal, then he returned to the shipyard. Although the prisoners continued to work for the next few days, when they showed up for work on August 13 they were told they could have the day off. Next day they received a meal which included meat, the first they had seen since their incarceration. On August 19 the prisoners learned that the War had ended. Jack Ford returned to Newfoundland where he lived for the rest of his life. He died in 1993.

Patrick Thomas McGrath

P.T. McGrath was born in St. John's in 1868. He completed school at age 14 and became a reporter for the newspaper *Evening Herald* in 1889. He also worked for the *New York Times* and was correspondent for the *London Times*. Although best known as a journalist, McGrath also took an active role in political life becoming assistant clerk in the House of Assembly in 1897, and later was appointed the Chief Clerk. He worked on behalf of Newfoundland in the French and American fishery disputes in 1898 and in 1912 was appointed to the old Upper House, the Legislative Council. In recognition of his services during World War I he was knighted in 1918. In 1924 P.T. McGrath undertook what was to garner him his greatest fame, as well as an honourary LL.D from St. Francis Xavier University and a fellowship in the Royal Geographical Society. It was McGrath who prepared Newfoundland's case in the Labrador boundary dispute, compiling a wealth of information which led to the dispute's being resolved in Newfoundland's favour in 1927. P.T. McGrath died in 1929.

E.J. Pratt

In 1945 Henry W. Wells of the Department of English at Columbia University wrote of E.J. Pratt as ''Canada's Best Known Poet'', while George Story, writing about Pratt in 1962, called him Canada's Greatest Poet. Edwin John Pratt was born in 1883 in Western Bay. He left school at age 15 and worked as a salesman and teacher. He left Newfoundland when he was 24 years old to attend university in Toronto. Pratt was 40 years old before he published his first book of poetry: *Newfoundland Verse*. Some of his best-known poems include ''Titanic'', ''The Cachalot'', ''Dunkirk'' and ''Erosion''.

Carl Frederick Falkenberg

Baron Carl Frederick Falkenberg was born in Botwood in 1897. When the first World War broke out he joined the First Division of the Canadian Expeditionary Forces and served at the Western Front. He transferred to the Royal Flying Corps as a pilot and by the end of the War had been wounded twice and had amassed 14 victories, for which he received the Distinguished Flying Cross and Bar. He retired from the Air Force in 1918 and went into the insurance business. Falkenberg died in 1980.

Robert Hayward

Bob Hayward was born in St. John's. At age 17 he distinguished himself by saving the life of a drowning man, an action which won him three medals. He enlisted in the Royal Canadian Air Force and was posted overseas in 1942 and on July 19, 1943 took part in his first combat. In May, 1944, Hayward was posted to 411 Squadron RCAF as a flight commander and on August 5 took command of the squadron. In September, 1944, Hayward was awarded the Distinguished Flying Cross. In November, after 195 sorties, Hayward ended his tour and received the Distinguished Service Order. He retired from the RCAF and joined Molson Breweries as a sales executive. He retired in 1980.

Patricia Murphy

Patricia Murphy was from Placentia. Her father, Frank Murphy, owned a general store there and published a small newspaper called *Murphy's Good Things*. Patricia's job was to interview relatives of people who died and to write up the death notices. In 1929 she left for New York where she planned to study music. She stayed with an uncle and, after realizing that music was not her calling in life, struck out on her own. She earned a few dollars playing piano at a restaurant near Columbia University and filling in for absent cafeteria workers. Before long she had saved up $60.

Patricia would often stop by a small restaurant called the Step-In. One day when she arrived she found the door closed and locked. She convinced the owner to let her in and over a cup of coffee found out that he'd been forced to close up shop. Patricia took over the restaurant and turned it into the

Candlelight Restaurant. That one restaurant grew into a chain of 10 restaurants and several gift shops around the United States. They were known for their elegance. Fresh flowers, china and a staff who made patrons feel pampered contributed to her success. Patricia Murphy was also known for her philanthropy and was awarded the rare Papal Honour of Lady of the Equestrian Order of the Holy Sepulchre of Jerusalem. Patricia Murphy died in 1978.

Robert William Boyle

"Billy" Boyle was born in Carbonear in 1883. He received his early education at Carbonear and at St. John's College. He was awarded the Newfoundland Jubilee Scholarship and went to McGill where he entered the electrical engineering program. His academic career was outstanding: Boyle won prizes, medals and scholarships and upon graduation he taught physics and mathematics at the university. In 1909 he was awarded the first Ph.D. granted by McGill, then moved on to Manchester where he continued work in radioactivity. He returned to McGill in 1911, then went to the University of Alberta when it opened.

When World War I broke out Boyle joined the Board of Invention and Research of the British Admiralty and was put in charge of work on detecting submarines by using high frequency sound waves. This method became known as Asdic (for the Anti Submarine Detection Investigating Committee). By the end of the War Asdic had been perfected to a range of 1400 yards. It was further developed during World War II and became an important tool in the detection of enemy submarines.

When the National Research Council Laboratories were established in Ottawa a director was needed for the Division of Physics and Electrical Engineering. Boyle took the post in 1929 and remained there until his retirement in 1948. During World War II, Boyle's group made several contributions to the war effort including work on radar. Robert William Boyle died in 1955.

James McKeever

James McKeever is the only person listed in the *Baseball Encyclopedia* as having been born in Newfoundland. Unfortunately very little is known about McKeever. Even though he's listed as being born in St. John's, Newfoundland, a search of local church records has failed to find a record of his birth — there is speculation that in fact he was from Saint John, New Brunswick. I tried several sources to track down more information about this man but to no avail. I mentioned my search to a friend in Washington State who is a baseball fan. He said he'd take a look through a computer program known as Total Baseball. This is what he came up with: James McKeever was born in St. John's on April 19, 1861. He played for Boston of the Union Association as a catcher and an outfielder. (The Union Association was a short-lived major league in the 1880s; McKeever was probably a local semi-pro player who suited up with the Boston Unions as a backup catcher for home games.) He played only 16 games, had 66 official at bats, had 9 hits and scored 13 runs. All of his hits were singles and he had no RBIs.

McKeever died in Boston on August 19, 1897. Obituaries in Boston papers of the time do mention that he was born in Newfoundland, although one says that he was born in New Brunswick. The Boston papers also note that he later had an extensive career as a minor league catcher, coach and manager in Minnesota.

Fanny Quinlan

In front of the CN Station on Water Street west stands a statue called "Industry". The statue is of a lady dressed in a long robe, her left hand resting on a cog and wheel. Newfoundland writer Kevin Jardine once wrote that the model for the statue was a young girl from Aquaforte, a Miss Croft who had been employed as a servant girl by Lady Reid. (The story of Miss Croft appears to be fascinating in itself in that Lady Reid thought enough of her to send her to the British

Isles to be educated so that she could become the Reid children's governess, and that she remained with the Reids for all her life.) That may be true, but according to most writers, the model for "Industry" was a young lady named Fanny Quinlan. Around the turn of this century Fanny was working as a maid for Charles Henderson, who was employed by the Reid Newfoundland Company as a stonemason — in building the railway station and in paving Water Street with cobblestones. Henderson was struck by the figure and height of this young lady (she stood 5 feet 11 inches) and decided to use her as the model for his work. Using a large pillar of stone that originally stood in front of the Station in St. John's, Henderson carved the statue. Each day Fanny would pose for two or three hours in Henderson's backyard, wrapped in an old curtain to simulate classical dress. The statue was unveiled in 1903 and has stood ever since outside the Railway Station building on Water Street West in St. John's. Fannie Quinlan married John Gushue of Whitbourne in 1906 and died in 1922, leaving five sons and one daughter.

Winifred Ann McNamara

Win McNamara was born Winifred Ann Shea in Pouch Cove in 1906. Although she was best known as a golfer, she was also a proficient curler. During the 1970s she won six provincial golf championships. For 15 years she was a member of golf teams representing the Province in national competitions and also served for eight years on the provincial golf association executive. She was the first woman to be inducted into the Newfoundland Sports Hall of Fame. Win McNamara died in 1980.

Eric MacKenzie Robertson

Robertson was born in St. John's in 1892. His claim to fame is that he was the first Newfoundlander to compete in the Olympics. Eric had done some distance running for the Newfoundland Highlanders Athletic Club and in 1920 found himself living in England where he was doing an apprenticeship in an English dry goods firm. While there he was invited to be a member of the British Marathon team which was to compete at the games in Antwerp, Belgium in 1920. He finished thirty-fifth. After he returned to St. John's Eric went to work in the family dry goods business, but he remained active in sports and was one of the people instrumental in organizing the Newfoundland Amateur Athletic Association in 1921. He died in St. John's in 1975.

Thomas David Dobbin (Dobbin the Diver)

Dobbin was born in St. Mary's in 1817. By age 18 he was master of his own ship, the *Hero*. When a schooner owned by a man named Smith McKay sank, Dobbin was called in to help with the salvage. (McKay has his own claim to fame, being one of the original partners in the Tilt Cove copper mine). McKay immediately saw Dobbin's courage and daring and asked him if he'd use a diving suit if one were provided. Dobbin indicated that he would. On one occasion while working on the salvage of the steamer *Kestrel*, Dobbin was relieved in his diving by another man whose name was Tremlett. Tremlett was in the water for only a short time when he began tugging frantically on the rope. By the time he got to the surface he was dead. Smith McKay was so shocked that he wanted to give up the job. Dobbin said no. He put on the dead man's diving suit and got into the water and finished the job. McKay then outfitted a schooner called the *Responsible* especially for diving and salvage.

Dobbin became a legend around Newfoundland and spent 14 years in the salvage business. (The best known story about Dobbin is told elsewhere in this book) He died in 1899.

Henry Supple

There were actually two well-known Henry Supples. Henry Sr. (known as ''Captain Harry'') was the leader of the sealer's strike of 1845. Sealers had for years been complaining about the money they had to pay to the ship owners in order to secure a berth to the ice. From 1838 to 1845 there had been a series of demonstrations and strikes. Then in 1845 Supple led a group of sealers from Conception Bay who had gathered in Brigus and refused to sail to the ice. The sealers won their protest. "Captain Harry" Supple later moved to New York with a family that included Henry Jr.

In late summer 1876, Henry Supple Jr. became the toast of New York. He was a master mechanic in the employ of Washington Roebling. Roebling's father was the engineer who designed the Brooklyn Bridge, but he died before the project was completed. Once the twin towers for the bridge had been erected on each side of the East River, Washington Roebling decided he had to get people interested in the undertaking, so he devised a publicity stunt. On August 14, 1876, the first steel wire was strung between the towers spanning the river. The word went out that on the 26th of August someone would attach a bosun's chair to the wire and ride across the river.

On August 26, thousands of people lined both shores of the East River and watched as Henry Supple climbed into the chair, a rickety contraption at best, and prepared for his 1600-foot trip across from Brooklyn to Manhattan. A fall into the river would most certainly have meant death and a few times it looked as though he would topple into the river. But Henry hung on and finally reached the other side, becoming the first man to cross the Brooklyn Bridge, albeit on one of the support cables. The bridge itself did not open for another seven years.

Shannon Tweed

Depending on what source you happen to be reading, Shannon was either born in Whitbourne (Markland Cottage Hospital), St. John's or Dildo in 1957. Whichever it happened to be, this much is certain, she IS a Newfoundlander, and she was Playboy Magazine's Playmate of the Year for 1982. She also became the magazine's first Video Playmate of the Month in January, 1982.

Shannon Tweed's father was a mink farmer at Blaketown, where she lived until the family moved to Saskatchewan in

1970. After she completed high school she moved to Ottawa where she became a waitress, competed in various beauty pageants and ended up co-owning a bar called Shannon's. She then became a model. After her appearance in Playboy Magazine as Playmate of the Month, she became publisher Hugh Hefner's companion. Eventually, though, the relationship broke off and Shannon turned to movies, ending up with roles in a number of low-budget films, as well as in TV series. At this writing Shannon Tweed is the companion of Gene Simmons of the rock group Kiss and continues to appear in movies and on TV.

John Vincent

Next time you pass Cochrane Street United Church in St. John's, take note of the design of the building. The architect was John Vincent of Cape Island, Bonavista Bay. Most Newfoundlanders have never heard of him — yet here was a Newfoundlander who was indeed world renowned in his day. He painted the portrait of a Pope and a King, and his paintings are in collections throughout the world.

Willie John (as he was known to his family) was born in Cape Island, Bonavista Bay in 1885. At an early age he, like most other Newfoundland boys, was fishing with his father. But Willie John's father saw that here was a boy who had a talent for other things, most especially drawing and painting. He even began designing homes for some of the people in Wesleyville, where the family had moved when John was seven years old. The elder Vincent had stashed away some money to get his son a proper education, so Willie John moved to St. John's. From there it was on to college at Boston Tech. During his college years John began to paint pictures of fishing boats. Whenever they were exhibited they were grabbed up by eager buyers. After graduation from college he went to work in Chicago but returned to Wesleyville for long enough to marry his childhood sweetheart, Violet May Carter.

Then, in 1912, the family returned again to Newfoundland for a short visit. While he was here Vincent discovered that a competition was underway for the design of a new Cochrane Street United Church, the previous church having burned down. Seven architects had been offered a thousand dollars each to design the structure. John approached the committee and offered his services. He said he'd like to submit a design for the building; for free. The committee accepted and when the results were announced John Vincent had won. Vincent didn't see the results of his design until many years later. Shortly after submitting his design he returned to the United States.

His fame as an architect well established, Vincent also began to make his mark as an artist. He painted portraits of many world-renowned figures. In 1924 he was commissioned to paint a portrait of King George V and the Queen. The painting was to be 27 feet by 18 feet and was to be used for the dedication of Liverpool Cathedral. Vincent later wrote about the feelings he had as he waited for the King and Queen to arrive for the sitting: "As the appointed hour drew near I became almost paralysed with nervousness and fear. Little wonder it is for I am only the son of a Newfoundland fisherman". Vincent's portrait, which took two and a half years to complete, was met with great acclaim. John Vincent was also probably the first non-Catholic artist to paint the portrait of a Pope. He had been selected from along 11 other painters to paint the portrait of Pope Pius XI. He also painted King George VI.

Although stricken with pernicious anaemia in 1943 and paralysis of both legs in 1945 which left him unable to paint for several years, he was determined to fight his disabilities and paint again. And he did. In 1961 John Vincent was invited back to Newfoundland to be a guest of the provincial government for the opening of the new campus of Memorial University. He died in New York in 1965.

Maurice Cullen

Maurice Cullen was born in St. John's in 1866. He was only three or four years old when his family moved to Quebec. Like

John Vincent, he showed an interest in art at a very early age, first as a sculptor. He studied sculpture in Montreal with Phillippe Hebert. When Maurice's mother died in 1888 she left him some money which enabled him to attend the École des Beaux-Arts in Paris. It was there that his interest switched from sculpture to painting. He left the École in 1892 and began landscape painting. In 1894 he made his first submission to the Paris Salon, and in 1895 became the first Canadian to be elected an associate of the Sociète Nationale des Beaux Arts joining the likes of Rodin and Degas. Later that year he returned to Canada and for the most part his artistic output from then on was of Quebec. In the first decade of this century Cullen made a couple of trips to Newfoundland where he painted landscapes. In 1909 on a visit he met and married a widow named Barbara Pilot, whose son, Robert William Pilot, later also became a noted Canadian painter.

During World War I Cullen was commissioned by the government of Canada to go to Europe to paint scenes of the War. Among those who were influenced by Cullen were the Group of Seven. Maurice Cullen died at his home in Chambly, Quebec in 1934.

Christopher Pratt

Christopher Pratt was born in St. John's in 1935. He started out in Engineering and Science at Memorial University and Mount Allison University before switching to Fine Arts. In 1955 he met Mary West who was also studying Fine Arts at Mount A. They were married in 1957 and moved back to Newfoundland. Then they moved to Glasgow where Pratt studied drawing, after which he completed his degree at Mount Allison. Upon graduation in 1961 he became the first curator of the MUN Art Gallery, but resigned in 1963 to pursue his own work. His first solo exhibition was at the MUN gallery in 1965, then he exhibited at Expo in 1967. His work has been displayed in many centres North America and Europe.

In 1980 Pratt offered his services to the Newfoundland government to design a new provincial flag. He submitted six designs, and on April 29, 1980 one was chosen to be the flag for the Province.

Maurice Prendergast

In 1938, *Time* magazine wrote a glowing article about how the city of Boston was finally recognizing two of its artist sons: brothers Maurice and Charles Prendergast. This was 14 years after the death of Maurice and while Charles was 70 years old. Charles was born in Boston, but while Maurice may have been an adopted Bostonian, he was in fact born in St. John's in 1859. Maurice and Charles' father was from Ireland and ran a trading post in Newfoundland. He used to make frequent trips to Boston to buy supplies and on one of those trips met a young lady from that city. They were married and she moved to Newfoundland with him. After Prendergast's business failed he and his wife took their baby son, Maurice, and moved to Boston. Even as a boy growing up in Boston, Maurice was interested in art and he would spend a lot of his time sketching women.

Maurice Prendergast became one of America's great impressionist painters. At first Maurice worked as an apprentice in a commercial art firm. By age 27 he had saved a thousand dollars, enough money to head for Paris to study painting. And he lived there for three years. To many of his friends and acquaintances Maurice was known as Mon or Monny and he was known to be a very quiet man. He became a member of a group known as the Eight, a group of U.S. painters formed in 1907 as a protest against the National Academy. Maurice would often write little notes on the back of his sketches and on one had written "The love you liberate in your work is the only love you keep". He was totally dedicated to his work, never married and lived with his brother Charles for the rest of his life. Maurice died at age 65 in 1924.

Thomas Scanlon

Or is that Scalon, or maybe Scanlan? I've seen it written a few ways. Whatever the spelling of the name, Thomas Scanlon made quite a contribution to the history of Newfoundland, as a matter of fact to the world. In 1861 the United States was in the midst of a terrible Civil War. The North wanted to abolish slavery. The South wanted to retain it. In England slavery had been abolished and people there tended to sympathize with the North. But many in English business circles were siding with the South, as southern cotton supplied many of the textile mills of England and a lot of English money had been invested there. When the English government gave formal recognition to the government of the Southern States, people in the Northern States were outraged and demanded that their government declare war on England. Feelings between Washington and London were becoming quite tense.

Now remember — this was prior to the landing of the transatlantic cable and mail could take a couple of weeks to get to North America from England. Messages could be telegraphed to the United States from here, but it first had to come by ship. On a June night in 1861 a ship named the *Prince Albert* slipped into St. John's Harbour. She was carrying a dispatch destined for President Abraham Lincoln — a declaration that the government in England had decided to remain neutral. The dispatch needed to be sent immediately, before some incident might provoke a war.

However, the telegraph line was down all the way from St. John's to La Manche, Placentia Bay — over 100 miles. Officials didn't know what to do. Then a young operator named Thomas Scanlon spoke up. He'd take the messages, go to La Manche and transmit them from there. The young Brigus man stuffed the dispatches in a knapsack and headed out by horse and wagon. At Kelligrews he hoped to get a sailboat. He found one but the wind wasn't right. So he set out by foot for Lance Cove (near Seal Cove, Conception Bay South) where he woke up a fisherman and asked for his help. The two men went by skiff to Brigus where Scanlon had hoped to find a horse. No luck. So he set out on foot again for Spaniard's Bay. There he found a horse and wagon to take him over the barrens to New

Harbour, in Trinity Bay. Four miles into the trip the horse went lame and Scanlon jumped down and headed off on foot again. At New Harbour he found four fishermen whom he asked to help him get to Rantem. But the wind came up again and they ended up landing short of their destination. One of the fishermen decided to go overland with Scanlon. It was seven miles over swamp, bog, underbrush and through heavy woods. When they arrived at Rantem they found themselves faced by an arm of water that had to be crossed. The ferry was on the other side and the ferryman couldn't hear their screaming and yelling. A mile down the shore they found a house where they borrowed a gun and fired it several times in the air. It caught the ferryman's attention and he came across and took Scanlon to the other side. Then Scanlon went on foot the remaining three miles across the isthmus of Avalon to La Manche.

In La Manche he found the telegraph apparatus was out of commission. Despite the fact that the building was swarming with mosquitos, Scanlon got the key in working order and began to send the message, as two young boys swatted the mosquitos away from him with boughs. When he had finished he sat back and waited for confirmation that the dispatch had been received. When the clicking of the sounder gave him the news he'd been waiting for Scanlon sat back and gave a sigh of relief. By his efforts, Scanlon may well have averted a war between Britain and the United States — one which certainly would have also affected the outcome of the American Civil War.

Daniel J. Carroll (and various other poets)

Someone called the Trivia Show one day and asked ''Who wrote the song 'A Heart Cry from the West'?'' I had no idea. The caller informed us it was a St. John's poet by the name of Dan Carroll. (Rev P. Sheehan wrote the music). I found that bit of information interesting enough to want to learn more about Dan Carroll. He was born in St. John's in 1865 and got his education at St. Patrick's Schools where he excelled in art. After school he went to work at Callahan and Glass, a furniture store, where he specialized in woodcarving. His work was so good that he was commissioned to do some of the carvings at the Roman Catholic Basilica, including a coat of arms which was given to Archbishop Michael Howley.

But Carroll had other talents. His caricatures and cartoons appeared in the *Evening Telegram*, and under the pseudonym Sonny Jim he submitted poetry to the newspaper. The poems he wrote in memory of well-known Newfoundlanders or in honour of their accomplishments were especially well known. Although most of his poetry reflected his love of Newfoundland, Dan Carroll's work went outside our borders, too. He wrote for such publications as *Chambers Journal*, *Donahue's Magazine* and the *Boston Traveller* in the United States. Dan Carroll died in 1941.

By the way, lest you think that Newfoundland poets never came along until the beginning of this century, think again.

In 1839, *Poems written in Newfoundland* by Isabella Prescott was published. She was the daughter of Governor Prescott. Isabella Whiteford Rogerson is considered to be one of our major poets, having published two volumes: *Poems* in 1860, and *The Victorian Triumph and other poems* in 1898.

During the 1860s and 1870s one of the standout poets was Patrick Power, also known as Paddy Poore the Poet. He was from Pokeham Path in St. John's. (A fine bit of alliteration there). Unfortunately, a lot of Poore's poetry was oral, and little remains on paper.

Alexander J.W. McNeily was a lawyer and scholar who lived from 1845 to 1911. He translated poems from Spanish and Portuguese into English and wrote original verse as well, a lot of which was humorous or satirical and published anonymously.

Another scholar of note who wrote in the same era was Thomas Talbot. He was connected with St. Bonaventure's College but became involved in local politics and was eventually elected to the House of Assembly as a Liberal. He also became High Sheriff for Newfoundland. Some of his poetry was noted for its pastoral quality, dealing with such subjects as the ''Logy Bay Valley'' and a little river that flows into Quidi Vidi Lake near Pleasantville (Rennie's River maybe, or perhaps the Virginia River?). Talbot also wrote one of the first novels to be written in Newfoundland, *The Granvilles* (a work which is set in Ireland).

Of all the Newfoundland poets who were prolific around the turn of the century, Maurice A. Devine is one of the most enduring. He was renowned for his humorous and satirical verse, and one of the best known was his ode about the Noonday Gun (published elsewhere in this volume).

And there was Johnny Burke, Archbishop Michael Howley and Rev. William Bullock and dozens of others. Unfortunately, not too much of the work of the early poets is readily available in print.

John Gallishaw

John Gallishaw was born in St. John's and received his early education here. After learning navigation Gallishaw decided to move to the United States where he attended Harvard University and the University of California. He also taught at both universities as well as at the University of Hawaii. Gallishaw was interested in creative writing and while serving during World War I wrote ''Trenching at Gallipoli; the personal narrative of a Newfoundlander with the ill-fated Dardanelles expedition''. Then he established the John Gallishaw School for Creative Writing in Cambridge, Massachusetts. During that time he contributed to *The Writer* magazine and some of his writings were later collected into two works which are still regarded as important guides in the writing of fiction. They were ''The Only Two Ways to Write a Story'' and ''Twenty Problems of a Fiction Writer''. His analyses of novels, plays and scripts got him involved in Hollywood and with the arrival of talkies in 1927 there came a bigger demand for script writers.

John Gallishaw found himself working for MGM, Paramount, Universal and Columbia Pictures Studios, and with some of the big names in movies: Clark Gable, Cary Grant, Nelson Eddy, Jeannette MacDonald and Robert Young. Gallishaw retired in 1955 and spend a lot of his time after that doing something he had learned in Newfoundland, boating.

Michael McCarthy

Mike McCarthy was born in St. John's in 1845. He received his education at Renouf's Academy on Duckworth Street and after graduation worked in the printing trade at the office of the *Newfoundlander* newspaper. Then in 1863, McCarthy's father, Charles, decided to take the family and move to the United States. They arrived in Boston in the fall of 1863.

The United States was in this midst of the Civil War and Michael McCarthy decided to enlist. He joined a cavalry regiment of the U.S. Volunteers, then became a member of a regiment under the command of General Philip Sheridan and before long had shown himself to be a man of great courage. By the end of the war he had been promoted to first lieutenant. After the War he drifted around the U.S. doing various jobs. He was a ranch hand for a time, worked as a printer, and even as a trader. But he'd become tired of civilian life and decided to re-enlist in the cavalry. He joined Troop H of the 1st Cavalry in St. Louis, Missouri in May, 1869.

McCarthy made no mention of his Civil War record, even though to withhold such information was actually against regulations. No one seems to know why he withheld the information, but he did.

Before long he rose in the ranks to become first sergeant. In 1877 war broke out with the Nez Percé Indians and, because of McCarthy's knowledge of small boats, he was placed in charge of the two boats that were to take the troops over the Salmon River at White Bird Creek, Idaho. On June 17, 1877, the 99 men of the First Cavalry moved down White Bird Canyon to attack the Nez Perce village. But the Indians had moved out and were waiting in ambush. At first the commander of the troops decided to fight his way through, but then had second thoughts and decided to retreat. McCarthy and six men were ordered to move to a hill nearby and cover the others as they retreated. The Indians attacked and McCarthy's six companions were shot dead. McCarthy himself crawled into the bushes and remained there quietly, waiting for the Indians to pass. One squaw, thinking he was dead, took his boots. McCarthy didn't move. After the Indian woman had left McCarthy crawled farther into the woods and waited till all the Indians had gone. Then he made his way back to his post where he was greeted warmly by his comrades, who had thought he was dead.

On July 11, 1877, Mike McCarthy was again in the thick of battle when he took part in the Battle of Clearwater against Chief Joseph, and in October was at Bear Paw, Montana when Chief Joseph surrendered to the Cavalry. Mike McCarthy was awarded the Congressional Medal of Honour, although it took 20 years before he actually received the citation and medal. McCarthy only stayed in the regular army for a couple of years after the Nez Perce Wars, then he moved to Washington state and settled down. But army life didn't leave him. In 1881 he became a first lieutenant in A Company of the Walla Walla Artillery, and eventually Colonel and Chief of Engineers of the Washington National Guard. He retired in 1905. Michael McCarthy died in 1914 in Walla Walla, Washington. One of his pallbearers was Miles Moore, a former governor of Washington Territory.

A portrait of Mike McCarthy hangs at the headquarters of the Washington State National Guard. General Otis Howard of the U.S. Army called McCarthy "one of the bravest men I have ever known".

Sir Henry Pynn

Mentioned briefly in *Newfoundland and Labrador Trivia*, Henry Pynn was born in Mosquito, near Harbour Grace, in 1770. His father, William, was a fish merchant and magistrate. For a while Henry worked as a clerk at Danson and Company and then achieved notoriety when he assembled a force of volunteer soldiers in the Conception Bay area.

In 1796 he was inducted into the British regular army. He served in Ireland during the Irish Rebellion of 1798 and obtained a commission as ensign in the 82nd regiment in 1799. He fought with the Duke of Wellington in the Peninsula Wars, where he distinguished himself and became the idol of the Portuguese regiment. He became a lieutenant in 1799 and rose to captain in 1805. He was made a major and served with the Portuguese army in 1809 and was promoted to lieutenant colonel in 1814. The honours flowed in. On the field of battle Pynn impressed his superiors so much that they conferred the Portuguese Military Order of the Tower and the Sword to him on the spot. He received several other honours from the Portuguese government and in 1815 became Sir Henry Pynn when knighthood was conferred upon him by the King of England. He became the first native-born Newfoundlander to receive the honour.

In 1841 Sir Henry was made a lieutenant-colonel in the British Army. Although he had long since left Newfoundland, Henry Pynn never forgot his roots and kept up a correspondence with his relatives in Mosquito right up to his death in 1855.

"Almost, but Not Quite"
Newfoundland Connections

Next to the folks from home who made good, a favourite subject of Trivia Show listeners are all the obscure and wonderful links of many famous individuals to Newfoundland. In my first book I made mention of the Newfoundland connections of John Williams, Danny Thomas, Bob Crewe and many others. Since then a few more have come to my attention. Some may be a bit too obscure for all but the most dedicated trivia buff (we'll grab at almost anything to claim it for our own), but they're still connections to Newfoundland and Labrador.

The Three Stooges, Milton Berle and Soupy Sales

What do all three have in common (along with dozens of other comedians)? They all have used the famous "Pie in the Face" routine as part of their act. And where did the idea for the Pie in the Face come from? Well, according to what I've been told, Newfoundland. And to be more specific, behind the old Newfoundland Hotel in St. John's.

Mind you, this was a baffler. I dug and dug and used every resource I could to try to get the full story, and I have to admit that I struck out. Even though I can't confirm it, I'm including the story here in the hope that someone, somewhere can tell me the name of the book that refers to this incident so I can consider it verified. Here's how I found out about it. Last year when I was promoting my first Trivia book, I did an interview with Ray Bellew. Ray was, at that time, the host of CBC Radio's "Weekend AM" program. During the course of the interview Ray hit me with a "Did you know..." question about how the 'Pie in the Face' originated here in Newfoundland. A vaudeville performer named Doc Kelly was visiting Newfoundland with his partner, a Scottish vaudevillian. One day they were behind the Newfoundland Hotel, standing in the doorway of a barn when a young fella walked up to the farmhouse and snitched a pie. The lady of the house caught him and tore a strip off him. Then she took the pie and smacko, right in the face. Everyone watching the incident went into hysterics. Kelly and his partner decided to use the bit in their stage act that night, and they got the same reaction. It became part of their act and it just grew from there. Soon it was known the world over.

It was a wonderful story. Ray told me that when he read the story in a book about Doc Kelly, he was so impressed that he immediately showed the book to a co-worker. The co-worker asked to borrow the book, and that was that. The book disappeared. Unfortunately, Ray couldn't remember the name of the book, or the Scottish vaudevillian or anything else. I've scoured vaudeville encyclopedias and I've searched through libraries all over the world. No luck. If anyone can help me verify this story, please let me know.

"My Fair Lady", "Pygmalion" and Henry Higgins

"My Fair Lady" is one of the best loved of all broadway plays. It was so popular that it was made into a movie. The story is based on George Bernard Shaw's famous play "Pygmalion". Simply stated, the storyline has Professor Henry Higgins taking a beautiful but uneducated young girl named Eliza Doolittle and turning her into a lady of sophistication. Not only did he have to change her mannerisms and style of dress, but he also had to change her manner of speech. "The Rain in Spain" rather than "The Ryn in Spyn", don't you know. The inspiration for Henry Higgins is said to have been Melville Bell. Melville Bell was the father of Alexander Graham Bell and during the mid-19th century lived in St. John's, where he served as a chemist at McMurdo's Pharmacy. During his stay here he taught speech and elocution. Some sources also suggest that the future inventor of the telephone was named after a Newfoundland sealing captain, Alexander Graham, who was a friend of Melville Bell's.

Carroll O'Connor

Another of those unexpected connections. The star of "All in the Family" and "In the Heat of the Night" had an aunt who lived in Newfoundland. And not just any aunt mind you, but one of the builders of Roman Catholic education in Newfoundland. Her name was Mary Bridget O'Connor. To the church she was known as Sister Bridget, and eventually Mother Superior. Mary O'Connor was born in Kerry, Ireland in 1857 and came to Newfoundland in 1883. Two years later she was professed as Sister Mary Bridget of the Sisters of Mercy. She taught at Littledale in St. John's until she moved to Burin in 1904. In 1914 she returned to St. John's and became Mother Superior of the Sisters of Mercy, and in 1925 she became vicar-general of the congregation. Her brothers and sisters had moved to the United States and settled in New York — among them, the family of Carroll O'Connor (whom Sister Bridget visited). Sister Bridget O'Connor died in St. John's in 1945.

Babe Ruth

I had always heard that Babe Ruth's first wife was a Newfoundlander, from Harbour Main to be exact. But according to Kal Wagenheim in *Babe Ruth: His Life and Legend*, she was from New Hampshire. Mind you, the Babe was notoriously poor with names and Wagenheim notes that Ruth himself said his bride was a Helen Woodring from Nova Scotia. Wagenheim, however, concludes that her name was Helen Woodford, and that she came from Manchester, New Hampshire. Babe married her when he was 19 and she was 16. They were wed on October 18, 1914 and were married for 15 years before Helen Ruth died. However, some parts of the story do ring true: Woodford is indeed a common family name in the Harbour Main-Holyrood area, while the early 1900s was a time when there was a lot of movement from that area to the "Boston States". If anyone can re-establish Helen Woodford as a Newfoundlander, please let me know.

John and Lorena Bobbitt

Can you believe it? There's even a Newfoundland connection here! One of the hottest news stories of 1993 was the story of this couple. Lorena had become a little tired of her husband's ways so she cut off a rather essential piece of his equipment and threw it into a field. It was found, and was reattached. The doctors who performed the miracle work were Jim Sehn and David Berman. Berman was a 36-year-old surgeon from of Toronto, and guess where he learned his technique. Yep, right here in Newfoundland. David Berman was surgical resident at MUN's medical school from 1981 to 1987. Today he's practising medicine in Charlottesville, Virginia.

"The Wabash Cannonball"

A classic of country and western music, the best known version of this song is by Roy Acuff. Even this song which is so associated with the U.S. Railroad has a connection to Newfoundland and Labrador. The original version of this song was called "The Great Rock Island Route" and showed up in 1882. The opening lines were:

> From a Rocky Bound Atlantic
> To a Mild Pacific Shore
> From a fair and sunny Southland
> To an ice-bound Labrador

Under the title "Wabash Cannonball", which first showed up around 1904, the lyrics got a slight rewrite:

> From a Rocky Bound Atlantic
> To the wild Pacific Shore
> From the sunny South bound
> To the isle of Labrador

And, in 1938, a version by the Delmore Brothers got another reworking of the lyrics:

> From the Rocky Bound Atlantic
> To the south Pacific Shore
> From the coast of Maryland
> To the ice-bound Labrador.

Roy Acuff recorded it and turned it into a million seller in 1942. By then the opening lines had become :

> From the Great Atlantic Ocean
> To the wide Pacific Shore,
> From the green ol' Smokey Mountains
> To the south lands by the shore.

Acuff may have had the big hit, but there have been other versions recorded and sheet music published which put Labrador in the lyric.

Lewis and Clark's dog

In May, 1804, Meriwether Lewis and William Clark set out from St. Louis, Missouri an expedition across the United States to the Pacific Ocean which was to last two years. Their mascot on the trek was a Newfoundland Dog named Scannon.

But Shannon was not the only Newfoundland dog with a famous owner: others include the dogs owned by Humphrey Gilbert, Robert Kennedy, George Washington, King Edward VII, King George VI and Queen Victoria. Bing Crosby used to breed Newfoundland dogs, while the movie "The Dam Busters" is based on a true incident where the British Air Force tried to blow up three dams in industrial Germany during World War II. The leader of the bombing squadron was Guy Gibson. Gibson had a Newfoundland dog named "Nigger".

Rockwell Kent

Rockwell Kent was an American artist who was born in 1882. In the early part of this century Kent was living on Monhegan Island in Maine, but was searching for a location to do his work which could offer, as he called it, "stark grandeur". He found it in Newfoundland. In 1914 he moved to

Brigus, set himself up in a small house and sent for his family: his wife Kathleen and their three children. The Kents were accepted quite warmly by the residents of Brigus but, before long, some people began to regard his clambering around hilltops and coastline as being a little strange. Obviously, they weren't too familiar with what an artist does.

But, it was wartime and almost any foreigner was regarded with a little suspicion. Then there was his box of ''tools''. Why was Kent so concerned when it disappeared in the sinking of a ship from Halifax? Maybe it was being used to make bombs! Then he made the mistake of singing songs by Schumann in the German language at a church concert and the suspicions grew. Kent's response was to tack a sign over the door to his workshop. It read ''Chart Room. Wireless Station. Bomb Shop''. Underneath was the drawing of a German eagle.

Before long a detective showed up. Kent described him as a bowler-hatted Nick Carter type detective. The detective wanted to see identification. Kent showed him some clippings. The detective said they could easily have been faked. Then the detective said he had heard that Kent had a room that no one was allowed to enter. Kent nodded and pointed to the door, but the detective didn't open it. Then the detective told Kent he looked like a German. Kent asked ''Have you ever seen one?''. The detective didn't reply. He suggested that Kent visit the Inspector General on his next visit to St. John's, then he left. The next time Kent was in St. John's he dropped in on the Inspector General and later described the meeting as brief and stormy.

On a sunny afternoon in mid-July 1915, Kent was chopping wood outside his house when two men approached. One was the local constable; the other a plainclothesman from St. John's. ''You are to leave Newfoundland at once'', the plainclothesman said.

''By whose orders?'' asked Kent.

''By order of the Inspector General'', was the reply.

The Governor of the time, Sir Walter Davidson, granted a reprieve to the Kents until such time as their children got over a bout of whopping cough. As they boarded the ship in St. John's harbour to leave the colony, the little bowler-hatted detective was there, counting the Kents to make sure they were all leaving.

The story would have ended there except that in 1967 when Premier J.R. Smallwood was poring over the papers of Sir Richard Squires, who had been Minister of Justice in 1915, he came across the Kent story. Smallwood dug some more and found that Kent was still alive and well. Smallwood recognized that an injustice had been done the artist so he wrote Kent and apologized and asked the artist and his wife to come to Newfoundland as guests of the Province. Kent accepted and in July 1968, arrived in St. John's where he was met by the Premier and given the royal treatment.

Later that year Kent wrote and published a small illustrated book entitled "After Long Years" which recounted the story of his eviction from Newfoundland and his eventual return. It was dedicated to Joseph R. Smallwood and only 250 copies were published. The first copy off the press went to 'Clara and Joe Smallwood'. Rockwell Kent died at age 87 in 1971.

Bill Cosby

Bill Cosby is one of the most successful people in show business — an Emmy award-winning television star with several TV hits to his credit. But from 1958 to 1960 he was right here in Newfoundland: as a petty officer serving in the U.S. Navy at Argentia.

Rob Butler

A baseball player for the Toronto Blue Jays, Rob himself isn't a Newfoundlander — but his father is and Rob Butler has warmly welcomed his "adoption" by Newfoundland baseball fans. Frank Butler was born and raised in the Butlerville/Shearstown area of Conception Bay. Rob was born in East York, Ontario on April 7, 1970. He grew up and got his education in the area. Rob was a talented baseball player who ended up becoming a member of the Canadian National Team and the Olympic Team and was eventually drafted by the Toronto Blue Jays.

He was a member of the 1993 World Series-winning Toronto Blue Jays, becoming the second Canadian (after Ron Taylor of the New York Mets) to play on a World Series Champion.

Bampflyde Moore-Carew

Most of you have probably never heard of Moore-Carew. I hadn't either until a couple of years ago. He became known as the King of the Beggars or King of the Gypsies. Moore-Carew was born in July 1693. In 1745, he published his auto-biography, *The Life and Adventures of Bampflyde Moore-Carew*, in which he recounted his years as a man who lived his life conning people or pretending to be someone else. Moore-Carew was a notorious liar, so virtually anything he said probably should be viewed with some suspicion. But he did his research when it came to pretending to be someone he wasn't. He made five trips to Newfoundland and while here he observed everything around him. On his return to England on one occasion he told people he was Aaron Cock, the son of a well-to-do planter in Newfoundland. When he indicated he wanted provisions and a fishing vessel several fishing captains questioned Moore-Carew to confirm his identity as Aaron Cock. They posed all kinds of questions and when finished were convinced he was who he said he was and offered him any support he needed. (One of the stories that convinced the interrogators he was Aaron Cock is related elsewhere in this volume under the section about Religion).

As Aaron Cock, Moore-Carew continued with this deception until he was recognized by a watchmaker in the town of Taunton. He was captured and imprisoned but released again after a couple of weeks. The last trip that Bampfylde made to Newfoundland from England was unplanned. He'd gone to Dartmouth and, learning that a Captain Avent was commanding a vessel which lay at anchor in the harbour, decided to drop by to pay his respects and wish the captain a bon voyage. The Captain, his wife, Moore-Carew, and some other well wishers were having a few drinks when the Captain asked Carew if he'd fetch his cane. Moore-Carew went to the Captain's cabin and as soon as he stepped inside, the Captain locked the door behind him. Moore-Carew was too drunk to notice what had really happened, so he sat down to wait for someone to come get him. Next thing he knew they were at sea headed for Newfoundland. Although he was quite annoyed with the Captain for pulling the prank on him, he settled in for the trip and was treated quite well, even to the point of sharing the Captain's quarters. But when they arrived Moore-Carew was determined to get back to England. He had taken a couple of fishing trips on the vessel and wasn't keen on the work so he deserted and headed for the woods, living off the land until he finally reached Trepassey about a week and a half later. Ever the con artist, he bluffed his way onto a vessel bound for England and returned home. Bampfylde Moore-Carew died in 1758.

Elisabeth Greenleaf

Elisabeth Greenleaf was born Elisabeth Bristol in New York City in 1895. In 1917 she graduated from Vassar College, majoring in English and Biology. Then in 1920 she offered her services as a volunteer teacher at the Grenfell Mission Summer School in Sally's Cove. Although she was somewhat apprehensive about her trip to a place she had never visited before, Elisabeth met some people on the trip over from the United States who convinced her that she was headed for a place she would like. On her very first evening in Sally's Cove, just after she went to bed she heard what she described as ''the most beautifully haunting melody I think I have ever heard, sung by three or four rough heavy boy's voices.'' This began Elisabeth Greenleaf's fascination with Newfoundland folk songs. She began to collect them and the following summer when she returned she collected 30 more.

Shortly afterwards she married and for a number of years her collecting was interrupted.

Then, in 1929, she once again returned to Newfoundland, this time with Grace Yarrow (later to become Grace Yarrow Mansfield) who was a trained musicologist, and the two set out to collect more of the folksongs of Newfoundland. In 1933 Harvard University published *Ballads and Sea Songs of Newfoundland* which is acknowledged as the first scholarly work in the area of Newfoundland traditional songs. Elisabeth Greenleaf died in Rhode Island in 1980.

Discovery

In school we learned that Newfoundland had been discovered in 1497 by John Cabot. We also learned that the Vikings under Leif Erickson had been here around 1000 AD. In fact, the Viking discovery can be confirmed more easily than the Cabot story in that archaeologists found the remains of a Viking settlement at L'Anse aux Meadows; Cabot didn't leave any trace of being here.

And even though the Vikings were probably the first Europeans to visit North America, Americans still celebrate Christopher Columbus's discovery of the New World. Columbus wasn't the first, as a matter of fact he may not have been third or fourth.

Some historians maintain that fishermen from Bristol were visiting Newfoundland waters as early as 1482. One of the reasons the discovery of the lands by these men from Bristol was not documented may have been because they wanted to keep it secret so that others wouldn't move in on their lucrative fishing grounds.

But there are even earlier "discoveries" of Newfoundland or Labrador, at least three other discoveries of the New Founde Land for which some documentation exists: the discovery by Saint Brendan the Navigator, by Prince Madoc of Wales and by John Scolvus.

Saint Brendan

Saint Brendan was the patron saint of County Kerry and was born around the year 500 AD. According to one story about this famous Irish monk, he may have set foot on Newfoundland soil long before even the Vikings. The story has it that St. Brendan and 80 followers built a large ship in the year 550 and two years later made a voyage across the Atlantic to a "blessed Isle". They lived there for four years and after a number of the visitors died from some unknown disease, the remaining twenty returned to Ireland. They told of seeing armies of Redmen on the mainland, but had never been attacked by them, even though they made frequent voyages in their large canoes along the shore of the island. More than one historian has equated the blessed Isle with Newfoundland, and some have even gone so far to identify the island as Marticot Island in Placentia Bay, which has the right "hourglass" shape.

Prince Madoc

Prince Madoc was the son of Owain of Gwynedd of Wales. When Owain died his sons battled over who was to be the new family head. Madoc wanted no part of the conflict so he outfitted some ships and, leaving the coast of Ireland behind, headed for the sea. But where did he end up? Some historians say Greenland, others say Florida, even Mexico. No one can seem to pin it down more specifically. So it may have been Newfoundland. The year was 1170.

John Scolvus

Historians have argued for over a hundred years about whether a Scandinavian explorer named John Scolvus explored the coast of Labrador in 1476, or possibly even as early as 1471. The issue first came up in 1859 when a German historian discovered some old maps which led him to that conclusion. No one paid any attention to it until 10 years later when another German historian disputed it. It got bandied around another little bit and then in 1886 Norwegian historian Gustav Storm examined everything he could find about Scolvus. His conclusion was that Scolvus visited Greenland, not Labrador. And so it went, argument and counter-argument, but most leaning towards Greenland.

In 1920 Sofus Larsen of the University Library in Copenhagen, Denmark offered his conclusion based on his research of a series of documents he had come across. Larsen found that a Scandinavian expedition had been set up to find new lands at the request of the Portuguese government.

Captain Diderik Pining was the captain of the ship, John Scolvus was the pilot, and among the people on board were two Portuguese men, Joao Vaz Cortereal (the father of the two Cortereal brothers who visited Newfoundland in 1500 and 1501) and Alvaro Martins Homem. They were there to represent the Portuguese interests.

Larsen determined that Pining and Scolvus probably sailed from western Iceland, visited the shores of Greenland and sailed south at least as far as Newfoundland. The Portuguese passengers named the area Terra do Bacalhao (Land of Codfish). Although a document on the voyage was prepared and circulated by Cortereal after the group returned to Portugal, it had been lost. So there is nothing which can clearly confirm that Scolvus and the others did visit our shores in the 1470s, and it remains a mystery, although in 1984, writing in the *Geographical Journal*, Arthur Davies provided evidence that there was nothing to support the Scolvus story, and that, in fact, there was no John Scolvus. Davies proposed that Scolvus was in reality John Lloyd, a Welsh shipmaster. The Scolvus comes from the German word *scholfuss*, meaning skilful or expert. Hence John the Skilful or John Scolvus. Davies' theory was simply that John (the Skilful) Lloyd was making voyages to North America in 1480, still before Cabot and Columbus.

Disaster

Newfoundland and Labrador have seen many disasters, both natural and man-made, and a number of books have been written on the subject. For this volume I'll concentrate on five of the most memorable. In this chapter the stories of the tidal wave at on the Burin Peninsula, the Arrow Air Crash, the Knights of Columbus Fire and the sinking of the *Queen of Swansea*. Another tragedy is covered in the Military section of this book: the sinking of the S.S. *Caribou*.

Tidal Wave

On Monday, November 18, 1929 an earthquake struck on the Grand Banks. On the Richter scale it measured 7.2 — classifying it as a major quake. It was severe enough to be felt throughout Newfoundland and even as far away as the northeastern United States and eastern Quebec. People in St. John's felt the quake around 5 o'clock in the evening and, although it may have rattled them a little, there was no severe damage. Within minutes life returned to normal, the earthquake providing not much more than a topic of conversation on this sunny autumn day.

Darkness settled in on the south coast. Then around 7:30 disaster struck. A tidal wave swept along the shoreline of the Burin Peninsula and the west side of Placentia Bay, ripping buildings off their foundations, tearing boats off their anchorage and sweeping homes out to sea. There was utter pandemonium. People didn't really understand how much damage had been done until next morning when daylight broke.

They saw houses out in the harbours, and timber and debris strewn all along the shoreline. One of the more tragic stories about the disaster was of a group of rescuers coming upon a half submerged house. In an upstairs window a kerosene lantern still burned. When they broke the window and entered the house they found a small baby still asleep in a cot. Downstairs, on the first floor, the baby's mother and three other children had drowned.

The wave had also destroyed the only method of communication with the outside world. Telegraph wires were down all over the Peninsula. And to add even more grief, the weather turned bad: rain, sleet and strong southeast winds lashed the area. It was only when the S.S. *Portia* arrived three days later that news of the disaster could be relayed to the rest of Newfoundland and a rescue effort to help the victims of the disaster got underway.

When the tally was in, 27 lives had been lost and there was almost a half million dollars in property damage. Forty towns and fishing villages had been affected by the disaster. Hardest hit were the villages of Point au Gaul near Lamaline (where several families had built their fishing premises on the flat point) and Port au Bras near Burin (where the shape of the harbour funnelled the onrushing waters into the village). It took years to help all the victims but even then, for many, their method of livelihood had been destroyed. The tidal wave had ripped up the sea bed, sweeping away the marine life and destroying the fishing grounds. It was a decade before the fishery on the west side of Placentia Bay rebounded.

Other Quakes

The earthquake that caused the tidal wave on the south coast was not the first to be felt in Newfoundland and Labrador. Nor was it our first or only tidal wave. Here are some of the others:

1755. An earthquake in Lisbon caused a tsunami (tidal wave) that swept all the water out of the Bonavista harbour basin for ten minutes, then swept it back in, much higher than it had been before, causing it to overflow several meadows. That event gave rise to the folk song "A Great Big Sea Hove in Long Beach".

1775. According to Judge Prowse in his *History of Newfoundland*, a terrific storm out at sea caused the water to rise 20 feet above its normal level resulting in considerable damage along the coast and the loss of 300 lives.

1809. Earthquake in Labrador. There is some dispute over whether it was of magnitude 4.4 or 6.5, and whether it was at Nain or offshore from the community.

1836. Labrador again. This time it was felt all the way from Hopedale to Nain. Thought by some seismologists to be offshore.

1857. And another in Labrador, this time at Hebron.

1864. Another incident where the sea withdrew, this time at St. Shott's.

1884. On the Avalon Peninsula, the intensity of this quake is believed to have been approximately 4.1 and the effects were felt most strongly between Harbour Grace and Heart's Content.

1940. Earth tremors were felt along the South Coast from Burgeo to Rencontre East, and flashes of flame were reported in the sky above Francois.

1956. A mild earthquake on the northern Avalon Peninsula.

1957. Another mild earthquake, this time near Grate's Cove.

1965. And another minor earthquake, this time felt on the tip of the Bonavista Peninsula.

1969. Two earthquakes that year. One was felt in Lewisporte, Grand Falls, Windsor and La Scie. The second was 35 km offshore from St. John's.

1971. An earthquake in the Labrador Sea, but not felt on land.

1975. A quake felt in Pool's Cove and Rencontre East.

1985. There were three earthquakes detected in that year near Buchans. Two were felt by residents, but the third, although it registered on seismometers, went unreported by people living in the area. Seismologists speculated that they may not have been quakes at all but rock-bursts in the mines.

The Arrow Air crash

On 12 December 1985, a chartered Arrow Air DC-8 aircraft lifted off Runway 22 at Gander International Airport. A few seconds later it smashed into the ground killing 248 American soldiers and eight crew members. The servicemen were part of the international peacekeeping force on the Sinai Peninsula. They were on their way home to Fort Campbell, Kentucky for Christmas.

In the gift shop at the Gander terminal many of the soldiers had picked up some gifts to bring back home. Ironically many of them bought a T-Shirt which said "I survived Gander, Newfoundland". The tragedy was the worst aviation disaster ever to occur on Canadian soil, and the worst in the history of the United States military. The crash of that Arrow Air flight began a controversy that has continued years after the crash.

Initially it was believed icing on the wings was what caused the crash. The Canadian Aviation Safety Board in its report of December 1987, said that the pilot's failure to have the ice removed was what caused the tragedy. Immediately people came to the pilot's defence. Even within the Board itself there was disagreement and some of members refused to endorse the Board's final report.

Officials of Arrow Air said that medical evidence gathered after autopsies on the victims indicated that some had died from inhaling hydrogen cyanide gas which occurs when certain types of upholstery burns in some airplanes. The officials said this would indicate that there was a fire in the cabin before the plane crashed, and that it was probably caused by exploding ammunition or flares carried on the aircraft. There was even speculation that terrorists had managed to put a bomb on the plane.

John Gallagher, a pilot with thousands of hours flight experience in DC-8s, wrote in *Canadian Aviation* magazine in May 1989, that in his experience and based on information gathered about the flight, his theory was that the reverse thruster on No. 4 engine had activated, and even though it appeared the flight crew had taken every step to try to correct the problem it was too late to recover.

Report after report came out, one disputing the other. Even former Supreme Court Justice William Espey, and George

Seidlein, who was the U.S. National Transportation Safety Board's chief investigator, discounted the icing theory. There was even talk of coverup in the whole affair.

Tragically, the real truth may never be known.

The K of C Fire

The night of December 12, 1942 was a cold winter's night in St. John's. At eleven o'clock people within the coverage area of Radio Station VOCM gathered near their radios for the live broadcast of "Uncle Tim's Barn Dance", a popular radio show, which was broadcast from the Knights of Columbus hostel in St. John's. The emcee was Barry Hope (whose real name was Joe Murphy). About ten minutes into the broadcast, Barry thanked singer Biddy O'Toole (Mary Bennett) for her song, and introduced a special guest, a Canadian Army Corporal by the name of Eddie Harris. Eddie was singing "Moonlight Trail" when suddenly a woman's scream could be heard above everything, then "Fire! Fire!" Barry Hope ran to stage front and shouted "Don't panic, folks". Then he turned to the members of the band and said "Play, boys. For God's sake, play". Then suddenly there was silence.

At the Hostel, there was pandemonium. The fire had spread rapidly, flickering up over the walls and across the ceiling.

Throughout the building people were looking for some means of escape and many put their own lives in great peril to save others. One of the survivors spoke of seeing a tall, strapping Canadian soldier grab patrons and throw them through the window to safety before falling back into the flames. For the fire department it was a hopeless task. From the time they received the call until they arrived on the scene, only about one minute had passed, but the building was an inferno and there was little they could do except keep the blaze from spreading to nearby buildings like the CLB Armoury.

Next day, people began counting the dead. Eighty service people (22 of whom were members of the Newfoundland Militia) and 19 civilians had died. Among the victims was "Uncle Tim's" son, Kevin Duggan.

An inquiry into the fire was set up with Judge Sir Brian Dunfield in charge. When all the witnesses had been heard and all the reports in, Judge Dunfield said he found no reason to suspect spontaneous combustion or faulty electrical wiring. One witness at the inquiry indicated that rolls of toilet paper with the ends pulled out and trailing down had been seen in a cupboard at the hostel. Similar rolls were discovered at another hostel some weeks later.

Also, another fire had taken the lives of four people at another local club on a night when a large military party was supposed to take place, but which had been postponed because of bad weather.

And, in Halifax, a man was apprehended putting a lighted cigarette in a letter box at the Knights of Columbus hostel.

In his report, Judge Dunfield said "I am of the opinion, although I cannot prove it at present that the fire was of incendiary origin". Certainly it was generally believed in St. John's at the time that the fire had been set by a Nazi saboteur.

The *Queen of Swansea*

Of all the stories of marine disaster around Newfoundland, few stir the emotions like the story of the *Queen of Swansea*, a ship from Swansea, Wales which travelled back and forth across the Atlantic. Although only a few lives were lost in the tragedy, the documents left by the victims give us a story of sheer horror and despair. The tale is related in great detail in *Shipwrecks of Newfoundland and Labrador* by Frank Galgay and Mike McCarthy, but I'll give a condensed version of it here.

On the morning of December 6, 1867, the schooner *Queen of Swansea* left St. John's headed for Tilt Cove in Notre Dame Bay. On board were Captain John Owens, the mate, a pilot they had picked up in Newfoundland, six other crewmen and six passengers.

On the morning of December 12, the ship foundered on the rocks at Cape John Gull Island in Notre Dame Bay. Eleven of the people on board managed to get off, four went down with the ship. But those who survived hadn't been able to save anything; no extra clothes, no shelter, no water and no food.

Across the bay they could see the lights of Shoe Cove, just eight miles away. The castaways lit fires with the scraps of brush they were able to find but it didn't attract the attention of the people of the community. One by one the people who had survived the sinking died from exposure, thirst and starvation. The fate of the people wasn't known until April 1868, when Captain Mark Rowsell of Leading Tickles was returning from a seal-hunting trip. Two of his crewmen landed on Gull Island in pursuit of a bird they had shot. There they found the bodies of the passengers and crew of the *Queen of Swansea*.

The horror of what the castaways had gone through was revealed in a series of notes which they had written. A note from one survivor, William Hoskins, indicates that they even resorted to cannibalism to try to stay alive.

There were also notes written by Captain John Owens, and another passenger, Dr. Felix Dowsley. The last note was written by Dowsley to his wife on Christmas Eve.

After the full story of what had happened came out, people brought pressure on the government to build a shelter on Gull Island and stock it with food so that if ever a ship foundered on the island again the people would stand a better chance of survival. Eventually a monument was erected to the memory of the 15 who had died.

Military

Newfoundland and Labrador has had quite a Military history, dating from the very early years when the French and English battled on our soil. In more recent years, World War II came right to our doorstep — with the sinking of the *Caribou* between Port aux Basques and North Sydney, as well as the sinking of other ships off our shores and in our harbours. But there are some aspects of our military history that aren't as well known, like the Nazi Weather Station in Labrador, the Victoria Prisoner of War Camp and Frank Bartlett's stone wall in Corner Brook. Here are a few notable events.

The Sinking of S.S. *Caribou*

On October 14, 1942, the War hit right at home when a German submarine sank the ferry *Caribou*. The *Caribou* was Newfoundland's transportation link with the mainland of Canada and for 17 years she travelled back and forth from Port aux Basques to North Sydney. She was built in Rotterdam, Holland at a cost of $600,000. She arrived in St. John's on 22 October 1925 and went into service shortly afterwards. The Caribou was 265 feet long, 2200 tons, had a crew of 46 and could comfortably accommodate about 284 passengers.

On the night of October 13, 1942, the passengers boarded the *Caribou* for the crossing from North Sydney to Port aux Basques. That night there were 73 civilian passengers and 118 service passengers. This with a crew of 46 made a total of 237 people. Only a month earlier, the *Caribou* had been fitted with extra emergency life rafts, a factor that probably helped save a lot more people than otherwise would have been saved. The *Caribou* was being escorted on that night by the HMCS *Grandmere*, a Bangor class minesweeper.

Around 3 o'clock on the morning of the 14th, the *Caribou* was struck on the starboard side by a torpedo. She was about 40 miles southwest of Port aux Basques. People rushed to the deck to find that the starboard lifeboats were of no use. They had been blown away by the force of the explosion when the torpedo hit.

Some of the other boats could be launched but only one on the port side made it to the water because of the heavy list as the ship started to sink. Life rafts, installed only a few weeks before, now became the best method of survival. People scurried around the deck in utter confusion and panic.

Meanwhile, the submarine that had torpedoed the *Caribou* surfaced, and the *Grandmere* gave chase and tried to ram her. *U-69* (or, as she as known to her crew, "The Laughing Cow") crash-dived to get away from the minesweeper which retaliated by dropping depth charges on the sub.

There was mayhem on the deck of the *Caribou* as the ship started to dip into the waves. It had only taken ten minutes from the time the torpedo struck until the vessel slipped under the waves. One raft from the *Caribou* was overloaded and broke up, spilling its occupants into the sea. Many people survived the actual sinking itself only to drown in the ocean or die of exposure in the lifeboats.

At 8:30 the *Grandmere* came back into view and began to pick up survivors. Of the 237 people who were on the *Caribou*, 103 survived although two of the survivors died on the *Grandmere*.

Sinking of the ore ships

In September and November of 1942, four iron ore-carriers were torpedoed while anchored in Conception Bay. Before the outbreak of World War II, a lot of the iron ore coming from Bell Island was being shipped to Europe, and much was destined for Germany. After the war broke out, the ore was being shipped to Canada and the United States for use in the war effort. Germany recognized the importance of this was material and decided to stop the shipments. It was generally believed that because some of the U-Boat commanders had captained German ore boats before the war that they knew the approaches to Bell Island and the waters of Conception Bay.

However Steve Neary, in a recent book about the sinking of the ore ships, debunks that belief and indicates that none of the U-Boat commanders who were involved in the Bell Island incidents was ever here before. Nonetheless, Bell Island was providing iron ore, a very important element of the War effort and Germany wanted it stopped. Military people in Newfoundland recognized the potential danger and imposed a blackout on the area. They also stationed a unit of the Newfoundland Militia on the island and military aircraft were on standby at Torbay.

On 5 September 1942, three loaded ore carriers (the *Saganaga*, the *Lord Strathcona* and the *PLM-27*) were at anchorage awaiting convoy. A cargo ship named the *Evelyn B* was about to discharge a load of coal. At about noon, two explosions were heard. The *Saganaga* had been struck by enemy torpedoes and sank in minutes. Because there was no warning there were heavy casualties. The *Lord Strathcona* was next, but her crew had gone into action fast enough to get away from the ship.

A customs motor launch was on her way back to the dock when the *Saganaga* got hit. She put about and returned to where the ore carriers had been struck and began to drag people from the water. Shore guns started up and the *Evelyn B* started to fire in the direction of the attack. By this time aircraft from Torbay were also into the thick of things, but the attack was over. When the tally was in 29 of the 43 crew members on the *Saganaga* died.

On 2 November 1942, the *PLM-27* and the *Rose Castle* were at anchor at Lance Cove, about a thousand feet from the beach. A smaller cargo ship, the *Anna T*, was anchored between the other two vessels and the dock. The *Flying Dale* was at dock loading. At 3:30 AM there was an explosion and flares were seen falling. Many people who saw it thought it was an air attack, but people near the action saw the real story. They were rocket flares from *PLM-27*, which had been hit by a torpedo. She had broken in two and was sinking. The *Rose Castle* was also torpedoed. But no one on shore saw it happen.

The *Anna T* was narrowly missed by a torpedo which hit the dock just a few feet from the *Flying Dale* which suffered only minor damage. In total, there were 93 men on board the *PLM-27* and the *Rose Castle* — 58 survived.

Ironically, clothing which had been presented to the Women's Patriotic Association by the crew members of the *PLM-27* after the sinking of the *Saganaga* and *Lord Strathcona* in September, but which was not needed at that time, ended up being used by survivors of the *PLM-27* herself when she was hit in November.

Nazi Weather Station in Labrador

On October 22, 1943 the German submarine *U-537* anchored at the entrance to Martin Bay in northern Labrador. Captain Peter Schrewe gave the order to unload. The cargo was put in rubber dinghies and taken to the beach. Schrewe knew that if he was attacked he would stand no chance — he couldn't submerge or run for it. But his mission was important. On the beach his men worked through the night assembling a transmitter, antenna and weather measuring devices. The operation took 28 hours. Schrewe checked to see that the 150 watt transmitter was functioning properly on its assigned frequency of 3940 kilohertz, then he slipped back out to sea.

Captain Peter Schrewe and his men had just installed a remote automatic weather station in Labrador. Every three hours the station would come on air and send two minutes of coded weather information to be received by stations in Europe. The Germans built a total of 21 of these stations, but this was the only one in North America. All the others were built on sites in the Barents Sea above Norway. The stations were to provide information about the weather in the North Atlantic for U-Boats operating there.

The station at St. Martin's Bay operated for two weeks before the signal was jammed by an unknown station. In 1944 Admiral Karl Doenitz decided to set up another station on the

Labrador coast but the U-boat sent out to set it up was sunk en route. For many years nothing was known of the weather station at St. Martin's Bay until some research by Franz Selinger of Germany and Alec Douglas, the official historian with the Canadian Armed Forces, uncovered the facts. On July 21, 1981 the two men visited the site and found the remnants of the station. Some of the canisters were still there, but what was interesting to Selinger and Douglas was that some of the damage done at the site seemed to have been systematic and had been carried out by someone who had been sent out to find and destroy the station.

Victoria Prisoner of War Camp

On June 14, 1940 the British government made an urgent request of the Newfoundland government. They needed some place to house civilian internees whom they considered to be security risks — people who, if Britain were attacked, might end up assisting the enemy. Several sites were considered: Heart's Content, Argentia, Port au Port, Whitbourne, Random Island and Victoria. Victoria won out.

The camp was constructed on an area of 600 by 1100 feet. It had 20 bunk houses, five mess houses, an officers' mess and quarters, three bunk houses for guards, a hospital building, electricity, and all the amenities needed, right down to the forks, knives and spoons.

So the camp stood ready to accept its inhabitants. Then on December 14, 1940 the Dominions Office decided it would not send any of its internees to Newfoundland after all. American authorities had expressed concern to the British about having these internees placed in such a strategic location as Newfoundland. They felt that with the country so close to the mainland, it would be possible for any escapees to enter the U.S. or mainland of Canada where they could become spies or saboteurs. With that possibility ruled out, the search was on for others who might use the camp, but to no avail.

In August, 1942, Britain decided it was time to dispose of the camp and use the money for the war effort. The Canadian

Forces in Newfoundland realized they could use the materials so they bought up everything and dismantled the facility by the spring of 1943.

It had never been used.

Bartlett's Wall

On Frank Bartlett's land in Petries, near Corner Brook, there's a huge stone wall. It was pointed out to me in 1986 when I was in Corner Brook on an assignment. I was being shown some of the sights around the area and my guide was Albert Colbourne (who at the time was the executive producer at CBC in Corner Brook). Albert mentioned to me that the wall had been constructed by some German prisoners of war who had been stuck in Corner Brook after being captured. But other than that there was almost no information available. I was fascinated by the story but everyone I talked to hadn't even heard of it.

When I started work on this book I decided that I had to know more about that wall. Finally I called Dr. Noel Murphy: I figured if anyone could shed light on a dim corner of the history of Corner Brook he could. He had never heard of the wall, but he was intrigued by it and told me "Leave it to me and if there's anything to it I'll be back to you in a day or so". Sure enough, two days later he called and said "I found your wall". He put me on to Frank Bartlett who gave me the whole story.

In 1914, when World War I broke out, there was a German ship in Corner Brook harbour. Authorities decided to seize the ship and put the crew, about five men, under arrest. The crew weren't thought to be dangerous, but they were to be imprisoned until they could be shipped off to the mainland for interrogation. Frank Bartlett's grandfather was the town constable, and recognizing that the men were hardly agents of the Kaiser, would let them out during the daytime. Then at night they would return to their jail cells.

The Germans would spend their time out jigging fish or whiling away the hours at some chore or another. When they learned that Chief Bartlett needed a boundary marker erected on his property they offered to do it to help pass the time.

They erected the marker, a stone wall some three hundred feet long, four feet wide, and from four to five feet tall. Large rocks were used along the exterior of the wall and smaller ones filled the inside. Some of the rocks, according to Frank Bartlett, have to weigh at least a ton, and he said he can't fathom how they ever managed to move them into place. Although some of the wall has been covered in by trees and brush, and a little of it has been damaged by children playing in the area, for the most part it is intact, a memorial to the work of a group of German prisoners of war who lived for a time in Corner Brook in 1914. Unfortunately, what happened to the prisoners themselves is unknown.

Bullets made of gold

This story goes back to another war: known in Europe as the War of the Spanish Succession this conflict stretched beyond Europe to anywhere that France and England had colonies (in the colonies the war was known as Queen Anne's War). Newfoundland was no exception, and at one point almost every populated area in Newfoundland was captured by the French. One interesting story from that era makes the Lone Ranger's use of silver bullets look like small stuff.

When the French settled in Newfoundland, they built as their capital a town they called *La Plaisance* (later to become Placentia). The governor at the time was a man named de Costebelle. Sometime during the winter of 1709-10 de Costebelle and a group of French soldiers (along with Micmac Indians) attacked St. John's. But the English garrison there was ready and they not only repelled the attackers but captured much of their weaponry.

In August 1710, de Costebelle was waiting for a fleet to arrive from France with fresh supplies, guns and ammunition. Then one morning the ship *Le Coureur* sailed into the harbour. But she was not what the governor had been waiting for: *Le Coureur* was on her way back to France with a cargo of gold captured from the Spanish. And she was being pursued by English warships.

Governor de Costebelle told *Le Coureur*'s captain to remove the gold and store it in the fort. Then the men, along with their weapons, were to join the garrison detachment, while the ship was beached. Next morning word came down from the lookouts on Castle Hill. Nine English warships were coming in.

The French prepared to defend their town. Even though its location provided a good natural defence, the fact that the soldiers were low on ammunition put them in a precarious position. Then the battle began. Throughout the day the French soldiers successfully defended their positions. But they were running out of ammunition. All the lead in the fort had been melted down into shot. The governor knew that another attack by the English wouldn't be repelled very easily. Then he had a bright idea. ''The English want the gold'', he is said to have declared. ''They shall have it.''

He gave orders that the gold was to be melted down into bullets. When the English attacked again, they were met with a volley from the French defenders of bullets cast from the Spanish gold. Driven back, the English knew it was pointless to continue and put back out to sea. The French had won, but at the expense of all the gold which had been destined for King Louis' coffers.

H.M.S. *Calypso* (later the *Briton*)

When I was a young boy growing up in Gander, every Sunday afternoon the family would bundle into the car and go for the traditional ''Sunday drive''. Now in those days (the mid- to late-1950s and early 1960s) the roads around Newfoundland weren't great, so about the best we could do would be to drive to Lewisporte and back. As we drove through Lewisporte in those years I was fascinated by the sight of a huge ship in the middle of the harbour. I had no idea where she came from or what she was doing there, except I had heard she was used to store salt. But I always wanted to know. I eventually found out.

Turns out that this ship was the *Briton*. That was her present name, but before that she was known as *Calypso*. She was launched in 1883. The *Calypso* arrived in St. John's in 1902 and went into service as a training and drill ship for the Royal Newfoundland Naval Reserve of the Royal Navy.

In 1914 she went to War, serving as part of the defence around the east coast of the Island. In 1922 she was decommissioned and sold to A.H. Murray and Company to be used as a salt hulk. In 1952 the *Calypso* (now the *Briton*) was taken to Lewisporte where she lay at anchor in the harbour for 17 years. Salt was stored on the vessel for use by the "floater" fleet. These floaters would come into Lewisporte and load up with salt from the *Briton* before they headed for Labrador.

When that came to an end, she remained at anchor in the harbour, a rusting hulk. When residents learned this once glorious ship was about to be taken to Embree, beached and then scrapped, some people in the area started a move to have the ship restored to her once glorious condition as a tribute to the men who trained and served on her. But they were unsuccessful.

A couple of tidbits

Newfoundland may have had the Newfie Bullet, but for service men serving at Harmon Air Force Base in Stephenville, a more famous train was the G.I. Trolley. This was a special "day coach" or trolley car adapted for used on Newfoundland's narrow gauge railway. The train could carry 45 passengers from the Quartermaster's Yard at Harmon Field to Corner Brook. It was used by servicemen wanting to visit Corner Brook.

Most history buffs probably know that the first troopship to come to Newfoundland during the Second World War was the *Edmund P. Alexander*, but what was the second? Answer: the *Leonard B. Wood*.

Argentia Naval Station/Fort McAndrew

The first meeting of Allied Leaders in World War II took place in August, 1941, at sea off Argentia. United States President Franklin D. Roosevelt and British Prime Minister Winston Churchill along with their Chiefs of Staff and naval and military commanders sat in conference for three days. It resulted in the Atlantic Charter which proclaimed the ideological goals of the U.S. and Great Britain.

Movies, Television and Books

MGM-Grand Studios

On a lawn at MGM-Grand Studios near Orlando, Florida there's a lifeboat, and written on the side of that lifeboat is "St. John's, Newfoundland". When a listener to the Trivia Show called one day to ask if I knew why it was there, I could only speculate that maybe it was there as a representation of the movie "Captain's Courageous". That may well be, but the actual craft itself is of more recent origin. I finally tracked down the answer through Puddester's Trading in St. John's. It turns out that the lifeboat is off the *Northern Cruiser*. Puddesters sold the vessel to a company in the Caribbean several years ago. The company refurbished the *Cruiser* and set her up for rental to reef divers. The lifeboat was sold to MGM Grand Studios who wanted it as a prop.

Get Smart

In episode 108 ("Shock it to Me") of the TV series Get Smart, the evil KAOS scientist Dr. Eric Zharko, portrayed by Tom Poston, finds a way to resurrect and control humans by harnessing electricity. Dr. Zharko works in a laboratory in a cave on a small island off Newfoundland.

MacGyver

One sharp-eyed television viewer who called into the Trivia Show one day caught a Newfoundland connection in this TV series, which ran for several years on ABC. He said that during the opening credits Dana Elcar, who played MacGyver's boss, stands with his finger pointing to a particular place on a huge wall map. The caller said it was Newfoundland. I had a couple of MacGyver episodes on tape and I decided to check it out. Sure enough, he's pointing to an area just off the south coast of the Island, by my estimation about 500 km south, on the Grand Banks.

Boys of St. Vincent

People often ask me who wrote the music for the movie "The Boys of St. Vincent", that famous made-for-TV movie based on the incidents at Mount Cashel Orphanage. It was written by Neil Smolar.

Roberta

A 1935 movie that wasn't exactly noted for its great plot, "Roberta" did give us some wonderful songs by Jerome Kern (like "Smoke Gets in Your Eyes") as well as elaborate dance sequences by Fred Astaire and Ginger Rogers. It also gave us a Newfoundland reference. One of the characters, John Kent (played by Randolph Scott), is described by his aunt as a "big, affectionate, blundering Newfoundland dog."

I Conquer the Sea

A 1936 release that I had personally never heard of before it was brought up by a Trivia Show listener, this film ran 68 minutes. The only name I recognize from the entire cast is George Cleveland, who had also starred in a number of "B" westerns. The movie is described as being a melodrama revolving around the Newfoundland whaling industry and the Portuguese population of the area.

Two Flags West

A 1950 western from 20th Century Fox, "Two Flags West" starred Joseph Cotton, Linda Darnell, Jeff Chandler, Noah Berry Jr. and Neil Rosenberg. Neil Rosenberg???

Neil may not be a native-born Newfoundlander, but he's lived here long enough that we can consider him an adopted Newfoundlander at the very least. A folklorist at MUN, Neil is the author of a comprehensive work on Bluegrass music called *Bluegrass : A History.* Locally, he's known by most people for his work with the Newfoundland bluegrass group Crooked Stovepipe, but in 1950 Neil was living in New Mexico. His father was working in Los Alamos.

At the time, Twentieth Century Fox Pictures was shooting "Two Flags West" in northern New Mexico at a native Pueblo village.

A call went out for extras to appear in the film. Neil's mother and a friend went to the casting call. During her interview Mrs. Rosenberg was asked if she could ride. She indicated she could, so she was asked to be the stand-in for Linda Darnell (as she resembled the star). Darnell wouldn't ride since her sister had been killed in a rodeo accident.

Neil and his brother were also cast as extras in the film. They had no lines to speak, but you can catch them in a brief appearance. There's a scene where the cavalry is riding into the fort. In the background a young boy and a girl are playing hopscotch. Neil Rosenberg is the boy. In the same scene a soldier is pushing another young boy across the screen in a wheelbarrow. The boy in the wheelbarrow is Neil's brother.

America's Funniest Home Videos

A show that is built on showing people's blunders, stumbles, bloopers and foibles, "America's Funniest Home Videos" recently featured a video from Newfoundland.

Wayne Haynes of Brother Rice High School in St. John's won second-place prize money ($3000) for something that happened to him at his graduation ceremony in April 1994. He was selected as the class clown by his fellow students and as he walked up the steps to the stage to get his award, he was watching his feet, making sure he didn't stumble and make a fool of himself. But he wasn't looking at what was above him. When he reached the top step he stood erect and his head smacked into a chandelier sending glass everywhere.

Goldfinger

In the movie "Goldfinger", Gander merely gets a mention when Bond regains consciousness in an aircraft and asks where they are. But, in the Ian Fleming novel on which the movie is based Gander plays a more important role. First of all, at one point, Bond is scheduled on a BOAC Monarch flight 510 from

New York's Idlewild airport (now Kennedy airport) to Gander and London. Then later, Gander Air Traffic Control comes into the picture to help the aircraft when it runs into trouble over the Atlantic during the novel's climax. Mention is also made of Goose Bay in that chapter as a possible alternate airport

Bits and pieces

Western movie star Tim McCoy was visiting Newfoundland quite some years ago and while he was here bought liquor at Churchill Park Liquor Store. He said "All the Rough Riders should shop here". The Rough Riders McCoy was referring to weren't Teddy Roosevelts' famous soldiers, but rather a trio of western 'good-guys' he was often associated with in his career. Two of the other 'Rough Riders' were Buck Jones and Raymond Hatton.

Here's a note I found stashed away in some files from some trivia shows of the 1980s: Mac Pike of Port Aux Basques was a stand-in for Freddie Bartholemew in "Captains Courageous". Pike later became manager of Canada Life.

According to J.R. Smallwood in volume II of the *Book of Newfoundland*, two of Hollywood's great character actors (William Farnum and Edward Everett Horton) got their starts in Newfoundland. Farnum was with the W.S. Harkins Company. Horton may be best known today for his voice-overs for the "Fractured Fairy Tales" and other segments on old episodes of the "Rocky and Bullwinkle" cartoons.

Night Over Water

Ken Follett, the author of several adventure novels such as *Eye of the Needle* and *The Key to Rebecca*, visited Newfoundland in August 1990 to do some research for a forthcoming book. One of the locations mentioned in *Night Over Water* (1991) was Botwood.

Tender is the Night

In this novel by F. Scott Fitzgerald chapter 13 begins with some of the characters — Dick, Rosemary and Abe — visiting the battlefield at Beaumont Hamel. As they walk through the trenches Dick comments on the bravery of the men who lost their lives there. As they come out of the trench they face a monument to the memory of the Newfoundlanders who lost their lives in the battle and Rosemary bursts into tears.

Peter Pan

In the book *Peter Pan*, by James Matthew Barrie, the Darling family dog is a Newfoundland. The well-known Disney cartoon movie, however, depicts Nana the dog as a St. Bernard.

Two other classic books mention Newfoundland (albeit in reference to Newfoundland dogs): *Moby Dick* by Herman Melville and *Far from the Madding Crowd* by Thomas Hardy.

Flo, Bob, David and Gordon

Flo Patterson, Bob Joy, David Ferry and Gordon Pinsent are four of our own who have gone on to become prolific actors in New York, Hollywood, Toronto and elsewhere. In *Newfoundland and Labrador Trivia* I gave you their biographies — in this volume, their filmographies. Made-for-TV movies are marked with an asterisk (*), while the name of the character portrayed appears in square brackets:

Flo Patterson

1989   *Lady Forgets, The [Rebecca's Mom]
1990   *Stephen King's It [Mrs. Kersh]
1990   Bird on a Wire [Molly Baird]
1991   *Captive
1992   *To Grandmother's House We Go [Grandma Mimi]
1992   *Man Upstairs, The [Mrs. Porter]
1994   *Seasons of the Heart

Robert Joy

1980   Atlantic City [Dave]
1981   Threshold
1981   Ragtime [Harry K. Thaw]
1981   *Escape from Iran: The Canadian Caper
1983   Amityville 3-D [Elliot West]
1985   Terminal Choice
1985   Desperately Seeking Susan [Jim]
1986   *Sword of Gideon [Hans]
1987   Radio Days [Fred]
1987   Big Shots [Dickie]
1988   Suicide Club, The
1989   Millennium [Sherman the Robot]
1990   Longtime Companion [Ron]
1990   *Judgment
1991   *Hyde in Hollywood
1991   *First Circle, The
1992   Shadows and Fog [Spiro's Assistant]
1993   *Woman on the Run: the Lawrencia Bembenek Story
1993   *Gregory K [Ralph Kingsley]
1993   Dark Half, The [Fred Clawson]
1994   Death Wish 5

David Ferry

1969   Three Into Two Won't Go
1989   . High-Ballin' [Harvey]
1981   *Whale for the Killing, A
1984   Bay Boy, The [Walt Roach]
1987   *Sadie and Son [Captain Ruggles]
1987   *Echoes in the Darkness [Don Reddin]
1987   3 Men and a Baby [Telephone Installer]
1989   Physical Evidence [1st Cop]
1989   *Day One [Army Major]
1993   *Woman on the Run: Lawrencia Bembenek Story
1993   *Woman on the Ledge [Billy]
1993   Strange Horizon [Pascal]
1993   *JFK: Reckless Youth (a TV mini-series) [Warfield]

Gordon Pinsent

1969   Colossus: The Forbin Project [president]
1972   Rowdyman, The [Will Cole] (also written by Gordon)
1974   Newman's Law
1979   *Suicide's Wife, The
1987   John and the Missus [John] (also directed)
1990   Blood Clan
1992   *In the Eyes of a Stranger (TV) [Lt. Ted Burk]
1993   *Bonds of Love
1994   *Due South [Sgt. Robert Fraser]

Extra! Extra!

While a struggling stage actor (read waiter) in London, Christopher Warrick of St. John's got a role as an extra in the 1982 Paramount film *The Lords of Discipline*, starring David Keith and Robert Prosky. The film, which is set at the fictional Carolina Military Institute, was so disliked by Southerners that the producers were forced to film it in England! Warrick and others playing first-year students at the academy actually had to endure drill and some "basic training" for the film.

Like so many great film performances, Warrick's one line in the film eventually ended up on the cutting-room floor — but he is clearly visible in one scene. In this scene a group of cadets are being drilled in a courtyard and some of the "knobs" notice the unsettling fact that one of their classmates is standing on the roof of one of the buildings. Despite orders from upperclassmen to keep their eyes front, the cadet played by Warrick glances nervously at his hapless classmate on the roof, and is reprimanded.

Business and Advertising

There are a lot of wonderful stories connected with some of our Newfoundland businesses and products. So, for this volume, I thought I'd include a couple of them, and also some of the catchy advertising slogans I've run across.

Newman's Port Wine

Most times we tend to groan about our Newfoundland weather. (The exception being the summer of 1994 which has to be the most fantastic summer ever, at least in my memory it is. As I write this, it's ten o'clock at night and 18 degrees outside). But even our usually cool, damp climate has a good side: it makes wonderful port wine. Some would say it's the best, and you can't duplicate it anywhere else.

In the fall of 1679 a ship owned by the Newman Company of England left Oporto, Portugal destined for London. A full cargo of port wine in casks was stored in the hold. As she headed into the Bay of Biscay, a French privateer gave chase and, to avoid capture, the Newman brig headed west. She evaded the privateer, but hit a storm. Eventually the ship ended up in Newfoundland waters and sought refuge in St. John's harbour. The vessel and her crew remained there for the winter. In the spring, she set sail again for England. When the ship arrived in London and the cargo was unloaded, it was found that the port had taken on a bouquet and taste that was unlike anything people had experienced before.

Officials in the company wanted to make sure, so they sent out another shipment of wine to Newfoundland to be stored and to see if it was the Newfoundland climate that had produced such a distinctive taste. The result was the same. So the company began storing much of their wine in their St. John's vaults.

Another interesting note about Newman's Port Wine concerns Napoleon. On July 15, 1815 Napoleon Bonaparte departed France for England on board Newman's vessel HMS *Bellerophon*. When the ship left Newfoundland for France in March she had on board 88 gallons of wine. So presumably Napoleon may have shared in some of the wine that was carried on board the vessel.

Newman's continued to store the wine in their vaults into the 20th century, and today the Newman & Company premises on Water Street at the foot of Springdale Street are a Provincial Heritage site.

Beaver and Jumbo Tobacco (and how we sell lobsters)

When we are doing the Trivia Show, the topics sometimes start to follow a thread. One thing leads to another, and then another, and so on. And so it was one afternoon when Anne Budgell and I were doing the show and we had a call from a listener who wanted to know if we knew what was different about the way merchants sold Beaver and Jumbo tobacco. Now I remembered distinctly what Beaver looked like: a block about four inches long, two and half inches wide and about three-quarters of an inch thick, if memory serves me. My paternal grandfather used to smoke it, and I remember him slicing off slivers of the tobacco, then crushing and kneading it between his palms before stuffing it into the bowl of his pipe. (Not the best-smelling tobacco in the world as I recall — I preferred my father's Holiday brand). But neither Ann nor I could remember what was different about the way Beaver was sold.

Both Beaver and Jumbo Tobacco were often sold by THE LETTER. Apparently the merchants would cut off the B in Beaver and sell it for 5 cents. Then the E and then the A and so on. Or you could buy a whole plug of Beaver for 25 cents. Same with Jumbo. Next question was "If you were buying your tobacco by the letter, when would you consider yourself very lucky?" The answer: when you bought the "M" in Jumbo — it's a wider letter.

That discussion had a couple of other callers telling about other Newfoundland items which were sold differently. For instance, do you know anywhere else that you bought potatoes by the gallon? And then we had a man call with a really interesting one. He started by telling the old Newfoundland joke about the tourist who asked the fisherman "How much does a pound of your lobster cost?"

The fisherman replies, "We don't sell 'em by the pound, we sell 'em by the each."

The tourist then asks, "Well how much are they each?"

The fisherman says, "$3.50 a pound."

How many after dinner speakers have you heard tell that one? But there's a logic to it, as the caller explained, something I hadn't even thought of before. Consider it. You can't buy a pound of lobster. They HAVE to be sold by 'the each'. But you have to know how many pounds EACH is before you can buy it. Made perfect sense.

Custard Cones

One day on the Trivia Show we got into a great discussion about custard cones, or soft-serve ice cream. Someone wanted to know if Newfoundland was the only place where they were called that — because whenever someone would ask for them by that name on the mainland they would get strange looks. However, in the United States, you *could* buy them as frozen custard. Then Jim Wellman, my co-host for the day, said to me "How about twirlies? Don't you remember when we used to buy twirlies in Grand Falls?" (Jim and I had worked together in private radio in Grand Falls). I said I hadn't. I don't know if I'd ever bought a "twirlie" in Grand Falls. I learned later that people in Lewisporte and Springdale also knew them as twirlies (or "twirly ice cream").

Then we had a call from a listener who told us that when soft serve ice cream first came to St. John's his father, Harold Power, had a small store near Rawlins Cross. He said many people believed that it was his father who had coined the term Custard Cones.

A caller to my office after the show pointed out that he used to buy them in Toronto as custard cones, but we speculated that maybe some of the thousands of Newfoundlanders who moved to Toronto were the people who originated the term there and maybe it really was a true Newfoundland name, something else we could lay claim to.

Just to make sure, I put out a call on the Internet, a worldwide network of computers with about 25 million users, to see if the term custard cones had ever been used anywhere else. One lady in Pennsylvania explained how in that state they have "frozen custard shops". And another chap, who didn't give his location, replied like this "In a time, long, long ago (about 30-40 years), in a land, far, far, away (the U.S. as it was then) what we now know as 'soft serve' ice cream was called 'frozen custard' and the stands which sold it 'custard stands'. It was often served in a paper dish, but, if you wished, you could order a 'custard cone'.

So I guess we can't lay claim to having "invented" the custard cone, but perhaps it is that (like so much Newfoundland speech) we have preserved a phrase which has died out elsewhere.

Cavell breakfast cereal

Cavell Whole Wheat Cereal was a product of the west coast during the 1930s. The wheat was grown and ground in St. George's, then produced as a cereal. Samuel Butt was the wheat farmer and after his death the cereal stopped being produced.

The box in which the cereal came had a picture of a little girl standing between two sheaves of wheat. The little girl was Sam Butt's daughter Cavell. The cereal even got an endorsement from the wife of the Governor at the time. She commented to Mr. Butt that his cereal was very good, but, she asked him, "Don't you think that it has a lot of laxative qualities?"

The Flying L Ranch

The Flying L Ranch was set up in 1961 by Saskatchewan rancher Harold Lees, when he saw potential for cattle ranching on the Burin Peninsula. In 1961 he brought in 125 head of Hereford cattle to Spanish Room. They came by train to Goobies then on a cattle drive down the Peninsula. In 1963 he formed the Flying L Ranch Company. In 1964 he brought in 1000 head of cattle, but Lees' plans to turn the bogland into suitable pastureland failed and hay had to be shipped in from Saskatchewan. Many of the cattle died, and many others were rustled by area residents. The venture eventually went into liquidation. Undaunted, in 1969 Lees again attempted the venture, but nothing came of it. In May, 1981, Lee's son, Grant, came to the Province and formed the Golden Bay Ranch Company but it too folded in February 1982. The only remnants of the Flying L Ranch today are vast, seemingly inexplicable fenced-in areas on the barrens of the Burin Peninsula.

Sally West

Any of us who watched television in Newfoundland during the 1960s and 1970s remember Sally West, the spokesperson for Cream of the West Flour. I think it's safe to say that Sally West, along with Bob Lewis, sold more flour in this Province than anyone else. There were the Cream of the West Christmas sing-a-longs, the contests, the commercials and the famous jingle that people remember to this day:

> Cream of the West Flour,
> Always the Best Flour,
> Always the best for your baking.
> Best flour in Newfoundland,
> Made just for Newfoundland,
> That's why whatever you're making...
> Try Cream of the West Flour,
> Always the best flour.
> Always the best for your baking.

I often wondered how many ''Sally Wests'' there were. I asked Bob Lewis, who told me there was only one. He also directed me to a couple of people, now living in Toronto, who worked with Cream of the West in those years when Sally West was the spokesperson.

They confirmed that there was only one Sally West: Ethel Whithem. Ethel was originally a resident of Toronto. When officials of the company saw the impact their spokesperson was having on sales in Newfoundland, they asked her if she'd consider moving to the Province. She said she would, and she became as much a Newfoundlander as any of us born here.

When Ethel passed away Cream of the West decided, out of respect, that the name Sally West would be "retired". Subsequent spokespersons for the company went by the name Mary West.

Browning Harvey Company

Before locally-produced hard bread came on the scene, Newfoundlanders used to eat hard bread imported from Germany, known as Hamburg Bread. In 1857 local baker Robert Vail developed a product which could compete with the imported one and before long it was the "hard tack" of choice. Vail made his fortune and retired to the United States, selling his "secret recipe" and mill to local businessmen. In 1873 Vail's Mill was bought by Gilbert Browning. The Vail-Browning mill was located on Water Street West, near the old Mill Bridge. In the 1980s the building was owned by Creative Printers and housed the offices of Harry Cuff Publications. Cuff found two millstones at the back of the property and mentioned it to Steve Herder, who arranged to have one of the stones donated to the city of St. John's. It was erected on the Rennie's River Walking Trail, to mark the spot where Rennie's Mill once stood.

Another businessman who became involved in the hard bread baking business was Alex Harvey. For years Browning and Harvey operated independently and in competition. Then in 1930 descendants of the two men merged the Harvey Company and the Browning Company to create one of Newfoundland's most successful businesses, Browning-Harvey Limited.

Purity Factories

Of course, these days if you mention hard bread (or peppermint knobs, lemon cream biscuits, cream crackers and syrup for that matter) there's one company that comes to mind: Purity Factories.

The company was started in 1925 by Albert Hickman, Calvert Pratt and W.R. Goobie. Today you'll find Newfoundlanders living in other parts of the world leaving standing orders with their relatives at home that whenever they come to visit make sure they have some of those products with them and to send a package of the goodies every Christmas.

Advertising Slogans

Writing a catchy slogan that people can remember is a real talent. And a lot of the slogans that came to represent Newfoundland and Labrador products and companies were, and are, as good as you'll find anywhere. As I researched this book I came across a lot of these old slogans and I found a lot of them quite intriguing. So, one afternoon on the Trivia Show, I decided to have the listeners call with slogans that they remembered. The response was beyond our expectations. Here are some of what we came up with:

Our Own bread baked by East End Bakeries was "Best by Taste test and best for you". The slogan was later shortened to the more memorable "Best by Test".

Purity kisses were "machine wrapped for your protection".

The Royal Stores believed in using a couple of slogans. It was called "The House for Value", and its motto was "Small profits-quick returns".

Ayre & Sons had a saying "You can get everything at Ayre's". The Ayre family were also prominent supporters of the Methodist Church, as were the principals in the firm of Steer Brothers, giving rise to a popular (if unofficial) slogan:

Be a good Methodist,
Say your prayers,
And buy your goods
At Steer's and Ayre's.

The Arcade Stores were "The stores where wise and thrifty shoppers love to shop".

Henley's Mattress Factory had you "Wide awake when you buy them, sound asleep when you try them".

The Standard Bedding Company, which was at the foot of Flower's Hill in St. John's in the 1930s, used an inverted triangle in its ads. On the left side of the triangle was the word "Quality". On the right side, the word "Service", and above the triangle "Invest in Rest".

J.M. Devine had a little store at 6 Adelaide Street.

When he moved to Water Street and opened a bigger store he called it "The Big Six". The store's slogan was "Once a number, now an institution".

Who can forget "Steer for Steers for all your insurance needs"?

But then, Arthur Johnson was "The Insurance Man".

And of course Munn's Insurance said, "You Can't Beat Munn's, B'y".

Brookfield Ice Cream in the 1930s was "The PICK-UP that never lets you down".

McMurdo's Drug Store had as its slogan "Dependable druggists since 1823".

Here's a slogan you'd never get away with in these times of political correctness — Household Movers & Shippers Ltd. used to refer to itself as the "Wife Approved Moving Service".

The slogan for Jackman and Green's grocery was "Up the line with Jackman and Green" (the slogan has not appeared on the storefront since a recent fire, but is still featured on the firm's delivery vans). A listener questioned what it meant so we checked. The current owners informed us that when the company was formed, in the early 1900s, Toby Jackman was an active soccer player. He took a soccer expression "Up the line" (which has to do with passing the ball up the line towards the goal and being a winner) and incorporated it into a slogan for his new business.

Browning Harvey's trademark was a partridge, their slogan: "The Taste will Tell". Not a bad slogan, but here's another slogan that the Browning Harvey Company used to advertise itself that has to be one of the dullest ever. The slogan claimed the company was "Sphinx-like in its permanence and dependability, through good times and bad". Try remembering that one. I guess, too, that they didn't realize that the Sphinx has eroded over time.

Wyatt's Coal "is better, that's why it sells the best". This was back in the thirties and forties when coal was sold in bulk, in lots of a quarter ton, or a half ton, or one ton or more. Tom Coady on Spencer Street had Coady's Coal. Their slogan was "Coady's Coal is good coal, 'cause Coady's buy from Wyatt's".

Remember you could always "Keep Cool with Keep Kool Beverages" and the company jingle was "Look for the white seal, Keep Kool".

Who can forget "Chug-a-lug-a-mug-a-Dominion" for Dominion Ale?

India Beer's jingle ran "India, India, India Beer/ India, that's the brew/ India Beer's the best there is,/ and it's all because of you."

H.W.C. Gillett Company of Twillingate were the agents for "the Tilley, the lamp that lights the province".

Pattie Crotty had a taxi business in St. John's back in the days when there were only three digits in the phone numbers.

Crotty's Taxi's phone number was 980. His slogan was "When and where you want to go/ call Crotty's Taxi, Nine-Eight-Oh".

Learning's Plumbing Company in St. John's had a jingle that went "Keep the home fires burning with Ventco Heat by Learning".

The Newfoundland Light and Power jingle was "I'm a real live wire/ and I never tire/ it is I who makes 'em hot./ I can cook your meals/ turn the factory wheels/ cause I'm Reddi Kilowatt". (By the way, a lot of people are under the impression that Reddi Kilowatt is a Newfoundland creation. Not so. Reddi Kilowatt was created for the Reddi Communications Company, which is owned by a man from Connecticut named Ashton Collins. The company is now based in New Mexico.)

One interesting bit of trivia concerning Reddi Kilowatt occurred when the New Democratic Party was getting off the ground in Newfoundland. At the time, Reddi was promoting conservation of electricity. The NDP took the logo, which showed Reddi flipping a switch off, and clipped it so that the most outstanding feature was Reddi's broad smile. They used the logo in some campaign literature along with the caption "You'd smile too if you made 14 million dollars last year". Newfoundland Light and Power decided to get their lawyers to investigate and see if there had been a copyright infringement. They learned that there wasn't. Reddi was now in the public domain.

William Drover had a mill on Temperance Street in St. John's. His slogan was "Sober service from Temperance Street".

In the 1940s, some St. John's companies would emboss their envelopes with a slogan reflecting their business. For example, Morgan Printing at the Board of Trade building offered "Every description of printing at moderate prices". Arthur T. Wood Company, a confectionary manufacturer and importer in St. John's said "Everybody loves candy". James Baird on Water Street was "The most satisfactory mail-order house".

Morrow's Nursery in Grand Falls-Windsor had the slogan "Come to Morrow for your flowers today".

Harvey's hard bread was advertised with the slogan "A cake a day keeps the dentist away".

Art Noseworthy Electrical said "Electricity is a work of Art".

The Premier Garment Company used to advertise itself with a jingle that was sung to the tune of "Alice Blue Gown". The lyric went :

> That's a sweet little Alice Blue Gown.
> Did you buy it somewhere in the town?
> So smart and so new, it looks lovely on you,
> Won't you tell where you bought it, please, I'm
> asking you.
> It's no secret, the whole town can see.
> From the Premier Garment Company.
> It has new style sensation, and what valuation.
> That sweet little Alice Blue Gown.

The Premier Garment Company also said "If your clothes are not becoming to you, you should be coming to us."

There was a haberdasher named Summers who used the slogan "The Smart Shop for Men."

Summers' location at this writing is occupied by William L. Chafe and Sons, also a tailor shop and haberdasher. The slogan for the business was "Clothes make the man, if Chafe makes the clothes". For a time William Chafe had worked for another tailor named Rosenburg. Then, in the early 1930s, he decided to strike out on his own. He moved to an upper floor in the Morris Building. At that time Tip Top Tailors sold their suits for $35. Chafe countered with the slogan "Climb the stairs and save 10" (his suits sold for $25).

Din Furlong ran a tailor shop on New Gower Street in St. John's, where he used to also dye clothing. His slogan was "We dye to live".

In Wiltondale, Bonne Bay there's a lumber company. On their business cards they have "Wiltondale Lumber, where a foot doesn't cost an arm and a leg".

Sung to a calypso beat by one of Canada's top female singers of the 1950s, Joyce Hahn, there was the famous jingle "Terra Nova Motors. Terra Nova Motors. Pontiac, Buick. Terra Nova Motors. Vauxhall, GMC Trucks. Terra Nova Motors. If you're looking for a new car, my friend, it's Terra Nova Motors we recommend. Now is the very best time to buy, and here is the man who will tell you why". (I've heard variations in the jingle including "If you're looking for a good car to buy, It's Terra Nova Motors, the one to try".)

In Bay Roberts, Mercer's Oh Boy Bread was "tasty, not wasty".

Saunders and Howell in Carbonear said "Prices born here, raised elsewhere".

Mona Ryan's Beauty Salon in downtown St. John's said "We'll curl up and dye for you".

Neyle-Soper Hardware had "Everything from a needle to an anchor", while Fort Amherst Seafoods had "Everything from a caplin to a whale" and the Horwood Lumber Company had "Everything from sill to saddle".

Gid Sacrey's business in Woodstock, White Bay — a typical Newfoundland outport general store — had, according to the slogan, "Everything from a baby's poop, to a clap of thunder".

Adler's Chocolate Bar was a locally-produced bar during the 1950s. One outdoor display pictured a large chocolate bar with the slogan "Adler's. What a block!" When it was advertised on CJON television, the announcer (whom our Trivia Show listener believed was Don Jamieson) would always end by saying "Man-Oh-Man, What a chocolate".

On their 80th anniversary Tooton's camera shop ran a newspaper ad which said the company was "Something to toot about".

The Lamppost in St. John's said "You'll see the light".

A St. John's man named Bobby Hudson used to buy bottles. He ran a store on Duckworth Street and then moved to King's Road. People used to say "Any bottles big or small,/ Bobby Hudson buys 'em all". (Bobby used to pay 5 cents for a large rum bottle, 2 cents for a flask, but also bought other kinds of bottles as well.)

The Thistle family have had a Flower Shop, which is called Thistledown, for about 35 years (as of this writing). Their shop is located in Corner Brook, while the greenhouse is in Steady Brook. The slogan is "If you can't grow flowers, try Thistle's".

Oliver. L. (Al) Vardy was one of the Broadcasting Corporation of Newfoundland's top announcers. His newscasts were sponsored by the Newfoundland Butter Company, and among their products was Solo Butter. The company invited listeners to come up with jingles to promote their products. One of the catchier ones ran:

The boy stood on the burning deck
Whence all but him had fled.
He had Al Vardy on the air
And Solo on his bread.

In the 1930s Imperial Tobacco of St. John's held a contest to come up with some new slogans for their products. The winner was for Gem cigarettes. It said "Seeking perfection? Make Gems your selection". Another entry said "For smokers' ease, say Player's Please".

One lady called in to tell how she'd entered some slogans in contests and won. For the TB Association she came up with "Dispel TB fear/ Have an X-Ray each year" and won a radio. For fire prevention she wrote "Fire prevention should be everyone's intention". For that one she won $25.

Not a slogan, but a saying from years ago in St. John's: Who was the lightest man on Water Street? Mr. Ayre. Who was the heaviest? Mr. Tooton (Two-ton).

The 1955 Corner Brook telephone directory had an advertisement for Lewis A. Young, who ran a radio repair business in Port aux Basques. The ad said "When your radio gets old, get Young".

Cinderella Flour was "Fit for a prince". One lady called into the Trivia Show to tell how her grandmother would bleach the flour bags and make various items of clothing, including underwear. Unfortunately, not all the writing would come out, and it wasn't unusual for a young lady, who happened to bend over, to show her flour bag underwear and for people to see "Fit for a prince" in bold letters across her backside.

The slogan for Harvey's Coal and Oil was "our customers are our warmest friends".

The Model Shop was "the shop where style begins".

Parker and Monroe were known as "the shoe men".

Spracklin's Building Supplies had "The Square Deal People".

"Red White and Blue means savings for you" was sung to the tune of "Hey look me over". The jingle continued: "Big travel bargains, all through the year. Here's all you do to save with Red White and Blue, pick the rate go CN".

On the Broadway in Corner Brook there was a clothing store called The Model Shop. They advertised that they were "exclusive but not expensive".

Advertising your undertaking business has to present particular problems when it comes to determining a slogan. You have to be very tasteful. One company in the Placentia area had as their slogan "We carry out what we undertake". Then there was the funeral home in Holyrood which also ran an ambulance service and catered weddings on the side. A sign outside the business read that they were in the service of "Hatching, matching and dispatching".

Geoffrey Carnell, the St. John's undertaker, was highly respected and used to attend the funerals of all the people he prepared for burial, no matter what the person's social or economic status. When Carnell decided to run for City Council, someone came up with the slogan "Geoff Carnell will be the last one to let you down".

On Humber Road in Corner Brook in the late 1940s or early 1950s there was a barber shop run by a man named MacDonald. In his window he had written "We need your head to operate. Cut down on your overhead and lighten up your face."

Peter Pan Sales asked people to "say Peter Pan to your grocery man".

OK Taxi in St. John's said "Have Cars will Travel".

The Bridgeway Motel on the west coast said "Check us out and we'll check you in".

United Nail and Foundry had a motto to "Make good goods, at a profit if we can, at a loss if we must, but always good goods."

In Pasadena there's a company called Honeywagon. They're in the business of cleaning out septic tanks. Their slogan: "We're number one in the number two business".

In Conception Bay South a company named Gas Tank Renew specialized in repairing gasoline tanks. Their slogan is "A great place to take a leak".

And finally, on the two days we ran our slogan extravaganza on the Trivia show, a few people called in with a rhyme about Carnation Milk. Carnation may not be a true Newfoundland product, but it has been seen in almost every Newfoundland kitchen. The listeners who called censored themselves because there are a couple of words in the jingle that would have been bleeped. But, for those of you who may have wondered what was left out, here's the rhyme in all its glory. There are several variations but they're all basically the same.

Carnation milk is simply grand
I always keep a can on hand.
No tits to pull, no shit to pitch,
Just punch two holes in the son-of-a-bitch.

Firsts, Lasts, Highests, Lowests, and other Milestones

This is the stuff that true trivia is made of — there is scarcely ever a Trivia Show that does not raise such questions as what's the highest mountain? Who was the first governor? That type of thing.

The hottest temperature ever recorded in the Province was 38 degrees Celsius. recorded at Goose Bay, Labrador. (Unfortunately, I haven't been able to find out the date. Must have been so hot they forgot to record it.)

Labrador also gets the distinction of having the coldest temperature ever recorded in the Province: -54 degrees C. recorded at Wabush in February, 1973.

The first snow plough used in St. John's was a converted World War I Whippet tank.

Tuna fishing in Conception Bay was a very popular sport during the 1950s and 1960s. The first tuna caught by rod and reel in Newfoundland was caught in 1938 by sportsman Lee Wulff who boated the 470-pounder in Bonne Bay.

Rainbow trout were first introduced to Newfoundland in 1887. They were imported from California and released in Long Pond.

Brown trout from Scotland were first introduced to the Province at Long Pond in 1884 by John Martin of the St. John's Game Fish Protection Society.

The most common tree on the Island is the Balsam fir.

The first female Members of Parliament from Newfoundland were Bonnie Hickey and Jean Payne. Both women were elected to the House of Commons in the federal election of October 25, 1993.

(Bonnie Hickey's mother, Isabelle Downey Ashley, was a former Miss Newfoundland.)

Chloroform was first used in the Province in 1848.

The first Chief Justice of Newfoundland was John Reeves.

The first courts of justice were established in Newfoundland in 1750, when Commissioners in Oyer and Terminer were appointed by British authorities to hear and make judgement on capital felonies committed in the Colony.

The first annexation of Labrador to Newfoundland was by Proclamation in 1763.

The first Supreme Court Bench in Newfoundland was appointed in 1826. It consisted of Chief Justice Richard Tucker and Justices John William Molloy and Augustus DesBarres. Later that year Molloy (described in Prowse's *History* as "a reckless, gay, squandering squireen") became the first judge to be removed from the Bench. In 1853 the former Newfoundland Supreme Court Justice was arrested in London for forgery. At the time the editor of the St. John's *Public Ledger* noted that this "notorious moucher" was "not wholly unknown... to a similar description of fame in the course of his residence in Newfoundland".

The first Prime Minister of Newfoundland under Responsible Government was the Hon. Philip Francis Little. He was 31 years old at the time, the youngest Prime Minister Newfoundland ever had. The youngest person ever elected to the Newfoundland House of Assembly was John Slade, who was only 23 when he became MHA for Twillingate in 1842. Bill Rowe holds the post-Confederation record, having been elected MHA for White Bay South in 1966, when he was 24.

Ask most people in the Province if they can name a Newfoundlander who was raised to the British House of Lords and you might get the answer "Edward Morris". And indeed the former Prime Minister was created the first Baron Morris of St. John's and Waterford on January 1, 1918. However there were two other Newfoundland-born Lords.

William Grey (Earl of Stamford and Baron Grey of Groby) was born in St. John's in 1850, while his father Rev. William Grey was president of the Church of England Theological Institution (later known as Queen's College). He returned to England at the age of three and had a distinguished career as an academic and administrator of charities before succeeding to the Earldom late in life, after the death of a childless uncle.

Oh yes, the third Newfoundlander to have sat in the House of Lords? That would be Michael, second Baron Morris and son of Edward P. Morris, who was born in St. John's in 1903.

The first steamers used in the seal fishery were the *Polynia* and the *Camperdown* in 1862. The *Polynia* is the subject of a well-known folk song, its name mis-pronounced as "the Old Polina".

The first train to travel across Newfoundland was in 1898 from St. John's to Port aux Basques.

Newfoundland was the first of Great Britain's Dominions to offer help to the home country at the outbreak of World War I.

Louise Saunders was the first woman to be admitted to the bar in Newfoundland in 1933. She had been a legal secretary with Sir. Richard Squires. In 1964 she became the first woman to become Queen's Counsel. She died in 1969.

Newfoundland's first female Doctor was Edith Weeks. She was born in Bay Bulls in 1882. After graduating from the University of Toronto in 1906 she returned to Newfoundland where she joined the staff of the General Hospital. She moved to British Columbia in 1910 where she met and married Henry Hooper. They moved to Australia and she continued to practice medicine until she retired in 1922.

The first female to act on stage in Newfoundland was Jean Davenport, in 1841. She was then 14 years of age. (Previously it had been the custom that all stage roles, including women, were played by men.)

Sister Mary Joseph Nugent was the first Sister of Mercy to be received in North America. She entered the order of the Congregation of Sisters of Mercy in 1843. Sister Mary Joseph is also considered to be the first woman to act as a nurse in Newfoundland.

The first professionally trained nurse in Newfoundland was Margaret Alexandra Rendell (later Margaret Shea) who began her practice in 1898.

In 1902, the first training school for nurses was established by Mary Meagher Southcott.

The first person to teach stenography and typewriting in Newfoundland was Sister Mary Joseph Fox, who began teaching the subjects in 1898.

The first women to run for public office in Newfoundland were Mary Kennedy Goodridge, Frances McNeill and Julia Salter Earle. They all ran for St. John's municipal council in 1925. They were all defeated, Salter Earle by only a handful of votes. Her campaign slogan was "Vote for Julia, she won't fool ya".

The first Brownie Pack in Newfoundland was started by Edith Mary Manuel in 1929.

Janet C. Gardiner became the first female chartered accountant in Newfoundland and Labrador in 1956.

Marie S. Penney became the first woman President of the Fisheries Council of Canada. She assumed the office in 1967.

Marion Pardy became the first woman to be made a deacon of the Newfoundland and Labrador Conference of the United Church in 1968.

In 1981, Elaine Ferris became the first woman deacon in the Anglican Church in Newfoundland.

In 1969, Dorothy Wyatt became the first woman to be elected to St. John's municipal council. She also became the first female mayor of St. John's in 1973, a post she held until 1981. Still a St. John's city councillor in 1994, Wyatt coined a memorable political slogan: "Vote for Wyatt, she won't be quiet" and also became known for her familiar greeting, "Hi, taxpayers". Of course, local wits soon suggested that salutation was really "High taxpayers", while potholes in the city streets became known as "Dottie's potties".

In 1973, Karen Quinton became the first Canadian musician to study at the Moscow observatory.

Hazel Newhook and Lynn Verge became the first women to become members of the provincial cabinet in 1979. In 1989, Lynn Verge also became the first woman to be appointed deputy premier.

In 1980, Dr. Marina Sexton became the first Newfoundland born woman dentist.

Christine Janes became the first woman full-time firefighter in the province in 1982.

In 1983, golfer and curler Winifred Ann McNamara became the first woman to be inducted into the Newfoundland Sports Hall of Fame.

Margaret Cameron became first woman to be named to the bench of the Supreme Court of the Newfoundland Appeal Division in 1983.

In 1983, Donna Hedges became the first woman to be employed on a drill rig off the coast of Newfoundland.

In 1985, Nancy Riche became first Newfoundlander to be elected vice-president of the Canadian Labour Congress.

Edith Cochrane became the first woman from the Province to be appointed to the Senate of Canada. She received the honour in 1986.

In 1992 Joy Burt became the first Newfoundland woman to become World Powerlifting Champion.

The first female photographer to open a studio in Newfoundland was Elsie Holloway who opened a studio in partnership with her brother, Bert, in 1913. Bert was killed during World War I and Elsie Holloway ran the business until the studio closed in 1946.

The first female mayor in Newfoundland was Dorothy Drover of Clarenville.

The first baby born in the province after Confederation was Sharon Rose Healey.

The first woman to cross the Atlantic in a balloon was Evelien Brink. Along with her husband Henk Brink and William Hageman, they lifted off from Feildian Gardens in St. John's (1985) and crossed the Atlantic in a record 51 hours and 14 minutes. An attempt the previous year had failed.

Newfoundland was Britain's first overseas possession. It was claimed on August 3, 1583 by Sir Humphrey Gilbert.

The first cornerstone in the world laid by remote control was laid at King George V Institute in St. John's by King George from Buckingham Palace on his Coronation day, June 22, 1911.

The first native-born Newfoundlander to become a privy councillor was Sir Robert Bond.

The first grammar school established by the Newfoundland School Society was opened in St. John's in 1799. Rev Lewis Amadeus Anspach was the first superintendent.

Canada's first heart/lung transplant was performed on a Newfoundlander, Jean Patey of St. Anthony, in 1985. She died on May 4, 1986, almost a year later. Her motto was "If you're going to die, at least die trying".

The first Newfoundlanders to be cited for bravery during the Korean War were Al "Duff" Lemoine of Grand Falls and Cecil Pelley of Botwood.

One day as I waited for our CBC Radio Building elevator to make the journey from the third to the first floor (a long, slow process) I struck up a conversation with a visitor who was also waiting for it. I commented that this had to be the slowest elevator in St. John's. The man turned out to be an elevator inspector and informed me that it wasn't the slowest, neither was it the fastest. He said the fastest elevator in the Province was at the Churchill Falls Power station. At one time it ran 1200 feet per minute. Modifications necessitated that it be cut back to 600 — it's still the fastest though. Hotel and high rise elevators usually run about 250 to 350 feet per minute.

The ultimate reference for most of these "bar bet" kinds of records is the *Guinness Book of World Records*. I decided to do a computer search through the electronic version of the book (1992 edition) and see what I came up with for Newfoundland and Labrador. Here's what I found.

On the subject of the Olympic Games, the longest journey of the Olympic torch in one country was for the Winter Games of 1988 which were held in Calgary. The torch arrived from Greece at St. John's on November 17, 1987 and was transported 18,060 km by foot, ferry or aircraft, snowmobile and dog-sled until its arrival at Calgary on February 13, 1988.

The greatest recorded amount raised by a charity walk or run is the 24.7 million dollars raised by Terry Fox who ran with an artificial leg from St. John's to Thunder Bay, Ontario in 143 days, from April 12 to September 2, 1980. He covered 5373 km.

Here's one that probably doesn't come as any great shock to us. The longest sea-level fogs, with visibility less than 1000 yards persist for weeks on the Grand Banks. The average is more than 120 days per year.

Harriet Holmes of Seldom Come By became the world's youngest great-great-great-grandmother on March 8, 1987 at the age of 88 years 50 days.

The earliest claim for transmission and reception of wireless signals across the Atlantic was made by Guglielmo Marconi, George Stephen Kemp and Percy Paget at 12:30 PM on December 12, 1901. The signal was transmitted from a 10,000 watt transmitter at Poldhu, Cornwall, England, and received at Signal Hill in St. John's.

The largest known invertebrate in the world is the Atlantic giant squid. The heaviest ever recorded was a 2.2 ton creature that ran aground at Thimble Tickle Bay (now known as Glover's Harbour) on November 2, 1878.

The first crossing of the North Atlantic by air was made by Lt-Cdr Albert Cushion Read and his crew in the 84 knot US Navy/Curtiss flying boat NC-4 from Trepassey Harbour via the Azores to Lisbon, Portugal from May 16 to May 27, 1919. The Newfoundland-Azores leg of the flight of 1930 km. took 15 hours 18 minutes at 81.7 knots.

The first nonstop transatlantic flight left Lester's Field in St. John's at 4:13 PM GMT on June 14, 1919 and flew the 3154 km to Derrygimla Bog near Clifden in County Galway, Republic of Ireland. The aviators were John Alcock and Arthur Brown. The flight landed at 8:40 AM GMT June 15, 1919.

The largest gorge under water is the Labrador Basin canyon, which is 3440 km. long.

And finally, according to the 1989 statistics of the American Kennel Club, in new registrations, Labrador Retrievers were the second most popular dogs with 91,107 registered by their owners. Cocker spaniels led the pack at 111,636.

Love and Romance

Almost everyone likes a great story of romance, and there are three in Newfoundland history which are outstanding. One is a real Romeo and Juliet story about a girl from Portugal Cove and her beau from Brigus, the second is the story of a girl from Fogo who found herself living with the royal family of France, and the third a story of the romance between one of the great British Poets and the woman who was to become the wife of a Governor of Newfoundland. Also I have another anecdote which I found written up in the *Newfoundland Quarterly* of Spring/Summer 1941. How true it is would be hard to determine, as a matter of fact the twist at the end may have you thinking "Oh, sure. Yeah, right". But it was too good to resist so I decided to include it.

The Story of Fannie Goff

Just inside the entrance to the old Anglican Cemetery at Portugal Cove there used to stand a headstone to Trypheny Goff. It stood there at least into the 1970s, but when I went searching for it during the summer of 1994, I couldn't find it anywhere. The inscription on the marker read "Sacred to the memory of Trypheny Goff, departed March, 1823. Age 22". This was a treasure that the people of Portugal Cove should have kept and displayed somewhere, for the story of Trypheny Goff is one of the most tragic love stories you could ever expect to hear.

"Fannie" was the daughter of Mr. and Mrs. George Goff, who ran a hotel in Portugal Cove. She had two nicknames: she was known to many as Pretty Pheenie, but to others she became Poor Fannie.

Fannie was beautiful; so much so that many who saw her considered her to be the most beautiful woman in all of Newfoundland. She was quite intelligent and could carry on a conversation with anyone and hold their attention, and she had a wonderful singing voice.

As you might expect Fannie had many suitors. At the time there were a number of military men stationed in the Colony who not only were taken by her beauty, but who also wanted to marry her.

Fanny wanted none of them; her heart belonged to a young man named Barter. He was a successful merchant who lived in Brigus. They courted for awhile and eventually set a wedding date, a day in March of 1823.

Two weeks before the wedding day Fanny was stricken with typhoid fever. Doctors rushed to her bedside from the city. But it was in vain. Fannie died, leaving a message for her prospective husband not to grieve for her.

In Brigus, Barter had no idea what had happened to his beloved Fannie. You must remember that this was 1823. There was no form of communication then which could have told him that his bride-to-be had died. So he was at home making preparations for the big event. He loaded his sleigh with gifts and set out on the trek to Portugal Cove.

On the morning of his planned wedding day, Barter reached what is now known as St. Philips. In those days it was known as Broad Cove. He stopped at the home of William Squires and asked if he might have some breakfast. The family realized that Barter had no idea what had happened. William Squires took Barter into the Parlour and broke the news to him.

Barter said nothing, he just got up and left. But instead of heading to Portugal Cove where Fannie was about to be buried, he returned to Brigus. Upon arriving there he set about putting his business affairs in order. Then he went to bed. He died three days later.

Fannie Goff was buried under an apple tree in her father's garden.

Pamela Sims of Fogo

In the spring of 1773 Nancy Sims (or Syms) of Fogo gave birth to a child out of wedlock. The father was Jeremiah

Coughlan, a naval officer stationed at Fogo who also had built up one of the largest trading concerns in northern Newfoundland. Coughlan had taken Nancy into his service. He appeared to be quite enamoured with her and said that he intended to marry her. After the fishing season was over in 1772 he returned to England. He returned the following spring and got a bit of a surprise when he found out that he was a papa. He took Nancy and his new daughter, who had also been named Nancy, into his house at Fogo and told everyone he would be taking them back to England with him and once there he would marry Nancy. They set sail but when they arrived in Poole, Coughlan deserted his wife and daughter. Nancy found herself in a bit of a bind, but managed to find a job in domestic service in Christ Church.

Meanwhile, in France, the Duke of Orleans had committed his children to the care of a Madame de Genlis. The Duke wrote a friend in London, a man named Forth, to say that he wished the services of a young English girl to be a companion for his children. Mr. Forth happened to visit Christ Church one day and saw the Sims' child. She was now six years old. Forth decided she would be the perfect companion for the Duke's children, so Nancy Jr. was sent off to France where the Duke's family fell in love with her. Madame de Genlis liked her new pupil so much she feared losing her. She travelled to England, found the elder Nancy and paid her 25 pounds to relinquish all claims to her daughter. Young Nancy was renamed Pamela and was educated in the same manner as her companions, the Prince and Princess. When the French Revolution broke out, the Duke sent Madame de Genlis along with the children to England for their safety. But before leaving a picture was painted of the family and hung in the Palace of Versailles.

Unfortunately when they arrived in London Madame de Genlis and the children had very little money and found the times very hard compared to the luxurious life they had been leading. They were eventually invited into the home of Richard Brinsley Sheridan at Ilseworth. Brinsley fell in love with

Pamela and they became engaged, but the engagement didn't last long and was soon broken off.

Then Lord Edward Fitzgerald entered her life. He had heard about this young girl from Fogo but didn't meet her until one evening at the theatre, when he spotted her and asked for an introduction. He fell madly in love with her and in less than a month they were married and settled down in Dublin.

Lord Fitzgerald and his bride were living a story book romance, they were in love, were living quite comfortably and, like all princes and princesses, they would have expected to live happily ever. But it was not to be. Lord Fitzgerald became involved with the Irish revolutionaries. He became their leader and a warrant was issued for his arrest. Authorities wanted to round up as many of these renegades as they could, especially the ring-leaders. On one occasion Fitzgerald narrowly escaped arrest when there was a raid on a house in which he was hiding. Several of his colleagues were captured, and although he escaped this time he couldn't avoid capture for long. Fitzgerald was eventually cornered by the authorities, and in the ensuing battle he was shot. He died a few days later.

Pamela was grief-stricken. She returned to the continent and went to live in Germany. There she met a U.S. Consul named Pitcairn whom she married, but the marriage only lasted a very short time, then they divorced and Pamela returned to France where she lived under the name of Fitzgerald.

Her former playmate, King Louis-Phillippe, and his family took no notice of the young girl who had lived with them and been their playmate and companion for so many years. Pamela moved to a convent in Paris where she died at age 55 on November 9, 1831. She was buried at Montmartre but in 1880 her grandson and grand-daughter removed her ashes to Thomas Ditton near London where they were placed in the family vault.

Carlyle's first love: Lady Bannerman

She was born Margaret Gordon on Prince Edward Island in 1798. Her husband was Alexander Bannerman, who served as governor from 1857 to 1863. Sir Alexander, or Sir Sandy as he was known to many, was considered to be a very fair man, a straightforward administrator, and one who enjoyed mingling with the people. He could be expected to rise to any occasion and act appropriately. His wife, Lady Bannerman, was a perfect match for her husband. She was a refined lady with a flair for singing and writing.

The two were married in 1824.

But Lady Bannerman had a secret she was keeping from everyone. Before she met her husband, Margaret Gordon had a brief relationship with poet Thomas Carlyle, one that left a lasting impression on him. When she was 19 years old Margaret met Carlyle at the home of her aunt, but it was another two years before they were formally introduced. Carlyle fell madly in love with this young lady who was four years his junior. In his autobiography *Sartor Resartus* he referred to her as Blumine. He said of Margaret "The first love which is infinite can be followed by no second like unto it".

But Margaret doesn't appear to have been as taken with Carlyle as he was with her and on June 28, 1820, two years after their formal meeting, she wrote him a letter in which she called off the affair. She said "When you think of me be it as a kind sister." She also told him that she wouldn't give him her address because she couldn't promise not to see him.

No one knew of the relationship between these two until after she died, when Carlyle in his Reminiscences identified her as his inspiration for Blumine. Aside from the references to her in his writing, Carlyle never spoke of Margaret after she said goodbye to him, and never did for the rest of his life.

The *Anglo Saxon* romance

On April 27, 1863, the passenger liner *Anglo Saxon* sank during a vicious storm near Cape Race. One hundred thirty-seven of the 444 people on board were rescued.

One of the people involved in the rescue was a man named Michael Green. Green was the grandson of an Irish refugee who escaped to Newfoundland after the start of the Irish

Rebellion of 1798. The refugee was named Michael O'Loughlin, but had changed his surname to Green. Michael Green assembled a crew of men and joined the rescue effort and he turned his home into a makeshift hospital to care for some of the victims. Seven people were survivors from the *Anglo Saxon* were brought into the Green home, even Green's daughter, Ellen, gave up her bed to two of the men from the ship.

One by one the survivors got back on their feet and headed to St. John's from where they would return home. All except one young man. Leonard Scott was in bad shape. It had taken days before he completely regained consciousness and the doctor had told the Greens that it would take a lot of care to nurse the young man aback to health.

As time passed Leonard began to fall in love with Ellen and she was quite attracted to him. One evening Michael Green asked his daughter to go for a walk with him. During the stroll he expressed his concern about the relationship he saw developing between Scott and Ellen. Green reiterated the hatred that existed in the family towards England and how if Ellen were to marry an Englishman it would not be taken lightly. Ellen assured her father that it wouldn't happen.

Michael Green headed for the fishing grounds off Labrador and while he was gone the romance between Ellen and Leonard Scott blossomed. Soon they were talking of marriage. Ellen's mother warned of Michael's ire if he should come back and find that his daughter had married an Englishman, but they decided to get married anyway. On the day of the wedding Michael Green returned from a trip to the fishing grounds in Labrador. When he learned of the marriage he was outraged. He said how he would never find forgiveness, but he would not harm the newlyweds.

A couple of days later while Michael and his new bride were walking along the ledge of the cliff where the rescue had been carried out, they rounded a boulder and came face to face with Ellen and Leonard. The newlyweds asked Michael for forgiveness. The father explained why he was against the wedding, how his hatred of England and the English would not allow him to ever consent to a marriage of any daughter of his to an Englishman. He said he disowned his daughter.

Then Leonard Scott began his story saying how he wasn't as much an Englishman as Green thought. Leonard explained how he, too, was the descendant of an Irish refugee who had fled to England after the 1798 rebellion. Michael Green's spirits were lifted. His daughter had married a man of Irish blood. He felt better. Leonard Scott went on to explain how his surname was not really Scott. The Scott name had been taken by his great-grandfather to cover up the family's roots. He went on to tell how his great grandfather had lost one brother in battle, and had become separated from his other brother when they were fleeing Ireland. Michael Green asked what was the original family name. Leonard said "O'Loughlin". His great-grandfather was Patrick, the brother who died in battle was Terrance, and the missing brother was Michael O'Loughlin. Not only was Leonard an Irishman by ancestry, but he was a blood relative of Michael Green. Green was overjoyed.

One little hitch presented itself. How would the church view this union, based on these new facts? The clergyman who had carried out the ceremony said in light of the fact that neither of the newlyweds were aware of their family relationship, and because it had been so many generations removed, he saw no problem.

A couple of days later, with everyone's blessing, Ellen and Leonard left Newfoundland on the *Shamrock*, which was on her way from New York to Liverpool, England.

Societies and Organizations

This is a continuation of a section on organizations included in the *Newfoundland and Labrador Trivia* book.

The Society for the Prevention of Cruelty to Animals

This group was formed in 1888 in St. John's. Lady Blake, the wife of Governor Sir Henry Blake was an ardent lover of animals and arranged a soiree at Government House to raise money for the new group. The society was then turned over to a committee of two, Judge George M. Johnson and the Hon. Daniel J. Greene. In 1912 the Society was reorganized and given a new name, the Society for Protection of Animals. At that time they hired an agent named Ernest Bastow to carry out their work. In 1914 the Newfoundland Legislature passed the Protection of Animals Act. The act was drawn largely from the British statute but it also drew from the laws of Canada and the U.S.

The inspector appointed by the Society in 1919, Jonas Barter, also had another trivia "claim to fame". Barter was an early convert to the Salvation Army and his marriage in 1891 was the first Salvation Army wedding performed in Newfoundland.

Total Abstinence and Benefit Society

The Total Abstinence and Benefit Society was formed in 1858 following a meeting called by St. John's blacksmith William McGrath at his forge near the base of the Hill O' Chips. McGrath brought a group of his buddies together and told them of his idea for the group. Other meetings followed and before long the group had decided on a set of rules which in essence said that the society's object was the "shielding of its members from the use of all intoxicating drinks and to afford relief in case of sickness or death: to elevate their individual characters as men and Christians." The society was properly instituted with the aid of John Little, a city barrister and brother of Prime Minister Philip Little, and members were required to take The Pledge. Their motto was "Be Sober and Watch".

As a sidenote, it's interesting that the women's movement took up the cause of abstinence as well in the latter part of the last century. In their publication *The Water Lily* they would publish lists of politicians who were abstainers and those who were not. The non-abstainers were accused of supporting and even profiting from "spreading death, destruction, ruin and degradation".

Community Concerts

The whole idea behind the Community Concerts Association was to provide people in small communities throughout North America with a chance to see good music at a reasonable cost. The Community Concerts Association came to Newfoundland in 1946. The organization came about when Victor Sutton, who was the manager of the Bowater's Mill in Corner Brook, heard a Metropolitan Opera artist give a community concert in a small town in Northern Ontario. He persuaded Community Concerts to add Newfoundland to their circuit and organizing director Albert Robinson was sent to Corner Brook to make a start.

People in Gander, Grand Falls, Corner Brook and St., John's became the first members of the organization. In St. John's there were so many members that there wasn't a hall capable of holding them all on the night of any particular performance, so each visiting artist had to perform his or her program on successive nights to squeeze everyone in.

In the first year the visiting performers were Jean Watson, Arthur Kent, and Nikolai and Joanna Graudan. The associations were strictly non-profit. The subscription cost to individuals was around $5 for three to five recitals each season. Any town which could provide a membership of 500 and a hall to hold them could become a member of the Community Concert family. The performers would receive exactly the same fee whether they appeared in St. John's or Grand Falls or any town anywhere on the circuit.

Society of United Fishermen

The Society of United Fishermen was started in 1873 by Rev. George Gardner, the Church of England minister in Heart's Content. It evolved from the Heart's Content Fisherman's Society, which Rev. Gardner had established in 1862. The aim of the Society was to help fishermen and their families in times of need. This could be something as simple as carrying water or wood or doing other essential jobs when someone fell sick. And they provided for a payment of a sum of money to widows in the event of the death of a husband. Each member of the Society would pay an annual fee which acted much like an insurance policy to assure that he or his family would be looked after in time of need. The Society built the first Fisherman's Hall in Heart's Content, and members, as a group, only met once per year. Business through the year was conducted by the officers.

In no time at all the organization had 250 members and for a time functioned quite well. But the numbers caused it to run into financial difficulties. In 1873 the Heart's Content Fisherman's Society evolved into the Society of United Fishermen. The group drafted a Constitution and Grand Lodge No. 1 was established at Heart's Content. Within three years 35 places on the Island had branches of the organization. In 1881 the Grand Lodge was moved to St. John's.

Although they had started as a group of people concerned for the welfare of their fellow fishermen, members also took an interest in the advancement of the fishery. They saw to it that improvements were made and abuses corrected. In 1875 the SUF set up a fish breeding station near Heart's Content, but it was not successful mainly because of its location. But it gave the impetus for the creation of hatcheries throughout the Island.

The SUF also was concerned with the moral fibre of its people. Its motto was "Love, Purity and Fidelity".

Temperance pledges were instituted in the lodges and Temperance Degrees were given in each lodge.

The organization received wide support. Church of England Bishop Edward Feild once said "There is No society which I would recommended our fishermen to join before the Society of United Fishermen". By 1923 there were 79 Lodges in Newfoundland and by 1928 Ladies's auxiliaries were permitted.

On its 100th anniversary in 1973 the SUF had five District Grand Lodges, 43 Ordinary Lodges in Newfoundland and one in Nova Scotia.

Society of Masterless Men

This is one of those exciting stories that I would love to have learned about in history at school instead of some of the stuff I was learning (or more correctly, trying to learn). It has adventure, excitement, romance and still gave a sense of what it was like to live in Newfoundland during the period.

In 1750 a deserter from the British Navy named Peter Kerrivan arrived on our shores. He'd had enough of the cruel life at sea. He hadn't wanted to join the Navy anyway, but had been pressed into service. When his ship docked in Newfoundland, Kerrivan and a couple of companions fled and headed for the woods along the Southern Shore.

They built shacks in an area known as the Butter Pots, near Ferryland. The Butter Pot was a hill located about nine miles from the harbour at Ferryland and which rose above the area providing the men with an excellent view all around them.

Soon other men from the area joined up. These were largely young fishing servants, who had been virtually sold to fishing masters in the area by merchant skippers. Their life was a bit better than Kerrivan and his friends had endured, but not much. Even the pettiest of crimes was met with great savagery.

The fame of the Masterless Men grew and their numbers increased. For the most part, they lived off the land but on occasion would sneak into the villages to trade with fishermen.

Some of the Masterless Men, including Kerrivan, even obtained wives from the settlements.

Authorities saw the Masterless Men as flagrant violators of the law and it especially irked them that, for many residents of the area, they were folk heroes. So the order went out. The Royal Navy was to track down these outlaws and round them all up. Then an example would be made of them with a mass execution. But even in those days the wheels of government and authority ground slowly. It took a number of years before any movement was made against Kerrivan and his men. By this time the group had become expert woodsmen and they were ready when an expedition of soldiers came looking. Kerrivan's band had constructed false trails throughout the forest and then headed further inland to hide out. After wandering around blindly for days, the expedition found the Masterless Men's settlement and destroyed it. Several other expeditions had the same results. On every occasion where the settlement was burned down, the Masterless Men rebuilt it. Only once did any members of the society get captured. Four young Irish recruits who had recently joined were captured when they became separated from the main group of men. They were taken back to Ferryland where a court martial was convened on the deck of an English frigate. The ship's company was summoned to witness the execution and the outlaws were strung up.

The Masterless Men were now more determined than ever to evade their hunters. They built their houses of spruce poles and bark so that nothing of value would be lost if they had to move quickly. And, ever ready to be on the move, they constructed roads and trails along the Southern Shore across the Avalon Peninsula.

Eventually as the times changed and people were able to lead an independent existence without being under the thumb of the fishing masters, the Masterless Men drifted apart, moving off to small coves and settling down. And so ended an era in Newfoundland history that had lasted for over fifty years. It's believed that Kerrivan himself never did return to civilization but lived out his years in the woods. He is thought to have had four sons and several daughters, so many of his descendants likely live on the Island today.

Unidentified Flying Objects

Ever since I was a boy growing up in Gander I've had this fascination with UFOs. Are they real? And if they are, where do they come from? Who's flying them? Some of my earliest non-fiction reading was in books about Unidentified Flying Objects. And, over the years, while my initial fascination may have waned somewhat, the interest has always been there. When I started work on this book I decided to dig out some information about some of the sightings around Newfoundland and Labrador. One of my favourite places for digging was on the Internet, that worldwide network of computers linking universities, schools, governments and commercial ventures. One night while ''surfing the 'net'' and doing some searches I came across something really interesting.

I found a document about Project Bluebook.

In 1974 the U.S. Military closed the files on Project Bluebook — the codename given to the military's investigation of Unidentified Flying Objects. Bluebook grew out of other projects: Project Sign had been set up by the American government in 1947. It was later renamed Project Grudge, and in 1952, Project Bluebook. The Bluebook files are blocked with information on UFO sightings, including ones right here in Newfoundland and Labrador.

In January 1974 a researcher for the Fund for UFO Research named Don Berliner went to Maxwell Air Force Base in Montgomery, Alabama to examine the files of project Bluebook before they were to be shipped to the National Archives. Berliner was planning on writing a book on the subject. He went through over 12,000 files and found among them almost 600 cases which have never been explained. Although investigators were often criticized for their eagerness to label cases as ''identified'' there were those few cases which they openly admitted they were unable to explain. Ten of them were in Newfoundland and Labrador.

The first of these unexplained sightings in our area occurred on July 10, 1947 at Harmon Field in Stephenville. Between 3 and 5 PM that day, three ground crewmen (including a Mr. Leidy of Pan American Airways) watched briefly while one translucent disc- or wheel-shaped object flew very fast, leaving a dark blue trail and then ascended and cut a path through the clouds.

At 1:30 in the afternoon on August 30, 1950 at Sandy Point, three local employees of the Harmon air base, including a Mr. Kaeel and a Mr. Alexander watched as a dark, barrel-shaped object with a pole extending from it down into the water, flew at 3-5 mph and 15-20 feet altitude for five minutes.

At 4 o'clock on the morning of April 18, 1952 in Corner Brook, a Mr. C. Hamilton, whose occupation was listed in the Project Bluebook files as a janitor, watched as a yellow-gold object made a sharp turn and left a short, dark trail during a one-minute sighting.

That same evening at 10:10, again in Corner Brook, a reporter named Chic Shave watched a round, yellow-gold object as it flew south and returned. Shave's sighting lasted a minute and a half.

On September 23, 1952 at Gander Lake, a group of people made an observation. An operations officer from the Fort Pepperell base and seven other campers observed a bright white light, which reflected on the lake, flew straight and level at 100 mph for 10 minutes.

Aside from these direct observations, many sightings have been made by radar operators, who have observed strange behaviour among blips on their scopes. On the evening of September 14, 1951 at 9:30, T/Sgt W.B. Maupin and Cpl J.W. Green were hunched over their radar scopes at the Goose Bay airfield when they saw two objects on radar. The two blips were on a collision course. One of the men got on the radio and barked out a warning. One of the objects evaded to the right.

The two objects were then joined by a third. The observation lasted more than 15 minutes. No aircraft were known to be in the area.

On June 19, 1952 at 2:37 in the morning at Goose Bay, 2nd Lt. A'Gostino watched as a red light turned white while wobbling. During that one-minute sighting an unidentified radar operator also tracked a stationary target.

One of the longest sightings in the Bluebook unexplained cases occurred on May 1, 1953 at Goose Bay. At 11:35 that evening the pilot and radar operator of a USAF F-94 jet interceptor chased a white light. For 30 minutes the object evaded interception and eventually disappeared from view. The entire incident was observed by a control tower operator as well.

Another chase in the skies over Labrador occurred on June 22, 1953 near Goose Bay. On that occasion, the pilot and operator of an F-94 interceptor chased a red light which was flying at an estimated 1,000 kts (1100 mph). After five minutes the object eluded the chasing F-94.

And at 11:25 on the evening of February 12, 1956 over Goose Bay, an F-89 pilot named Bowen watched helplessly as a green and red object rapidly circled his aircraft. The one minute episode was observed on radar by an operator named Crawford.

By the way, for those of you who may wonder about the term "Close Encounter of the Third Kind"... and, if there IS a Third Kind, is there also a First and Second Kind. Yes! In fact there is a Fourth and Fifth, too. Dr. Allen Hynek, the world's best known "UFOlogist", coined the 'Close Encounter' term, and decided its parameters. By his definition:

A Close Encounter of the first kind is an observation of a UFO within 150 yards.

A Close Encounter of the second kind is the finding of physical evidence that a alien craft or race exists.

A Close Encounter of the third kind is a visual sighting of an alien being or race.

A Close Encounter of the fourth kind is an abduction of an individual by an alien being or race.

A Close Encounter of the fifth kind is a direct contact or communication with an alien being or race.

General Trivia

Dobbin the Diver and the *Commerskie* (or was that the *Monasco*?)

Of all the stories I have tried to gather information about, none presented as many problems as this next one. And the reason it gave me so much trouble was that there are two versions of it, and each has been embellished and added to over the years — so that now it's reached the point that you just wonder what's true and what isn't.

Archbishop Howley wrote of it in his famous "Newfoundland Name Lore" series. P.K. Devine wrote of it. And so did Kevin Major, Jack Fitzgerald and Robert Parsons. There were others as well, and almost all the versions differ in some respect. I'll give both versions of the story.

The first version is set on a bright spring morning in 1855 when residents in the small Southern Shore community of Bigley's Harbour watched as a boat containing eight men and a woman came into the harbour. The newcomers said they were the Captain and crew of the S.S. *Commerskie*. The woman said she was the Captain's wife. They said their ship had run aground during the night and had sunk, and that the 71 passengers on board had drowned. People were shocked at the news. Eventually, the survivors returned to England but the story of the disaster lingered in the minds of the residents of Bigley Harbour. By now suspicions were beginning to surface, especially in light of the fact that none of the bodies had floated ashore. The residents began to suspect something was wrong with the story that had been told by the *Commereskie*'s survivors. Diver David Dobbin was called in to go down on the wreck. His first discovery was at the main-mast. A blonde-haired woman had been lashed to the rat-lines of the main-mast. She was wearing a red dress and blue blouse or coat. Her hair swayed in the water current. Nearby, four men were bound to the rail. Dobbin surfaced and told of his discovery, then he dove into the waters again. When he reached the passenger quarters he found the door had been nailed shut from the outside. He forced the door open and stepped into what must have sent a chill right down through his body. The room was filled with the bodies of the remaining passengers, men and women — some with their mouths gaping, their eyes staring. Dobbin tied a rope to each of the bodies and sent them to the surface.

The local police sent a report of what they had found to the police in England. The captain and crew along with the surviving woman were taken into custody and charged with murder. They were put on trial, convicted, the men hanged and the woman sent to prison.

The story that came out was that the ship had been under charter to a number of wealthy Dutch people who wanted to go to America. They asked the captain of the ship to look after their money and valuables. Among the passengers was a beautiful woman who fell in love with the captain, and he with her. They plotted to get rid of his wife who was also on the ship along with all the passengers. The crew were brought in on the scheme and together they all plotted to sink the ship on a part of the Newfoundland coast noted for its shipwrecks and where the water was very deep.

Interesting story, isn't it?. But a couple of problems: nowhere could I find a Bigley's Harbour (or Bigley's anything for that matter). And some versions of this tale put the sinking on the Southern Shore, the so-called "graveyard of the Atlantic" but not a particularly remote area by Newfoundland standards. Then there was a problem with the ship herself. In spite of a thorough search at the Maritime History Archives at MUN, there was no record of a *Commereskie* or *Commerskie* or *Commeraskie* (I'd seen it spelled all those ways).

But, we did find that there was a *Monasco*, that sank off Corbin's Head on the Burin Peninsula in 1857. That set me searching again, and this time we came up with something a bit more concrete.

The best retelling of that story is in Robert Parsons' *Wake of the Schooners*, so I'll only touch on the basic facts here.

On July 21, 1857 around 3 AM a ship named the *Monasco* sank at Silver's Cove near Burin. Captain Andrew Daly, a woman whom he said was his wife, and the crew (22 people in all), rowed ashore at Corbin, a small settlement near Burin, and told how they had strayed off course and sank. The ship was on her way from Gothenberg, Sweden to New York with a load of iron ore, and about 50 passengers.

The captain claimed that the passengers refused to leave their cabins to rescue themselves, and that they had barred their doors to keep the water out.

But the story sounded a bit fishy to the residents. They felt the passengers could have escaped just as easily as the crew. The captain and crew left the area a few days later headed for St. Pierre and from there to the U.S.

Several days after, the residents of Corbin decided to call in Davey Dobbin to dive on the wreck. On his first dive he found the doors to the passenger area were nailed shut from the outside. Dobbin dove again and pried open the doors, one by one. He sent 50 bodies to the surface. The bodies were buried in an area known as Swedes Point.

It was believed that the passengers had given their valuables to the captain for safekeeping on the way to America. Also, that the captain had fallen in love with a beautiful female passenger and decided to kill his wife and run away with his new woman. People figured Daly decided to sink the vessel near shore and clear out with the money and the woman.

On July 30, 1857 residents of Burin wrote the *Public Ledger* newspaper in St. John's asking the captain to come forward and prove the rumours untrue. He didn't. It was believed Daly went to the United States where he lived to a ripe old age with his lady.

How much of this story is true and how much is now legend, and which of the tales holds the most truth may never be known. One day after I mentioned the story on the Trivia Show, I had a call from a resident of the Burin Peninsula who was a recreational diver. He told me he had gone down to the area in question and had found bits of pottery and an anchor. Nothing else remained.

But, was it the *Commerskie*, or was it the *Monasco*, or was it something else? We'll probably never know.

The Hermit of St. John's (or was that Bay Bulls?)

Here's another widely-told story that has been documented so poorly that the true details have probably been lost to history forever. Which one of the versions of this one is true? Or, are any of the versions true? Maybe they're just figments of someone's imagination which have been wound into a story so often told that they're now related as fact — a phenomenon which has been recently described as "urban legend".

This is the story of the Hermit: He came to Newfoundland sometime in the 1860s. He managed to survive by selling trout to people in St. John's, and about six or seven years after his arrival he left. And when he boarded the ship to leave St. John's he was dressed in the finest of clothes, wore fancy jewellery and looked every bit the gentleman.

But the rest of the facts are very murky. According to Joe Smallwood as the Barrelman, the Hermit arrived in St. John's in 1868 and lived in a tilt on Topsail Road in St. John's, about a mile from Bowring Park.

Then there's a version which says that the Hermit lived in a hut on Bay Bulls Road, and that he arrived from England around 1868 and left by the S.S. *City of Halifax* to return home six or seven years later. This version of the story has it that he was about 45 years old when he left. It also indicated that people in St. John's later learned that the Hermit was from a distinguished family in England. He had left home to avoid having to marry a woman he didn't want (his father had reportedly arranged the marriage to unite two upper class families).

And then there's another version that says he arrived in St. John's just after the assassination of President Lincoln, and that many people believed he was John Wilkes Booth or was in some other way involved in the assassination conspiracy. According to this version, he lived in a cabin across the road from Bay Bulls Big Pond and returned to the United States only to be arrested and hanged for a murder he committed some years before.

Yet another version puts the Hermit in a tilt on the Dixie Line, off Brookfield Road, and asserts that when he left people searched his tilt and found various curios and expensive items.

There was even speculation that the Hermit was in fact Kevin O'Doherty, an exiled Irish patriot. But later investigation of O'Doherty revealed it couldn't have been him.

So who knows. Whichever it is, either version is interesting enough and has lots of mystery and intrigue.

Count de Courcy

Here's another of Newfoundland's more mysterious characters. The Count de Courcy, as he was known, arrived in St. John's in the 1880s. His dress and manner indicated he was a man of good breeding and one who was well-travelled. The Count claimed that he came from French nobility and that his god-parents were Pope Pius IX and the Empress Eugenie, the wife of Napoleon III. He claimed he was married to a lady whom he always called "Madame La Countesse", but that he had to leave France because of family and political reasons.

In addition to his native French, he could speak English, Italian and German fluently. He also possessed a wonderful singing voice and one evening at a St. John's auditorium he delighted the crowd, first with a rendition of the French National Anthem "The Marsellaise", then with the Welsh song "Men of Harlech", and then the Irish tune "Wearin' of the Green" — for which he received a standing ovation.

At first the Count seemed to be self-sufficient, and he spent a lot of his time searching for treasure and travelling with other men to places like Placentia, Chance Cove and Little Bell Island — trying to find pirate gold. And he always dressed well — the finest of clothes. But as years went by the clothes became tattered and his boots worn right through the soles. Presumably it was at this stage in his career that the Count found some employment with the boot and shoe business operated by David Smallwood (the grandfather of the future Premier). J.R. Smallwood's autobiography notes that de Courcy's job entailed writing doggerel verses in praise of Smallwood's boots:

Smallwood's Boots for lads and lasses,
Smallwood's Boots — they suit all classes.
Smallwood's Boots they are so grand,
They are the best in Newfoundland!
Smallwood's Boots are the best of leather,
Smallwood's Boots they suit all weather.
Smallwood's Boots they are so grand,
They are the best in Newfoundland!

Then, one cold and blustery Christmas Eve he showed up at a St. John's banquet hall looking like anything but a member of nobility. Some of the people attending took pity on him and brought him food and drink while he warmed himself by the fireplace. Then, with the wind whistling outside, he started to tell a story of a Christmas he had spent in Algiers. The contrast of the cold, stormy Newfoundland night with the tale of warm breezes, starlit skies and the smell of flowers enthraled his audience.

It wasn't long after that night the Count de Courcy fell ill with a cold and was taken to the General Hospital. He was diagnosed as having a pulmonary disease and died a few days later. In his delirium he kept calling out to "cherie Jacqueline" and "dear Madame La Countesse". The Count de Courcy was buried in Mount Carmel cemetery in St. John's. Unfortunately, no tombstone was ever erected to mark the spot.

Finnegan

Finnegan was another of Newfoundland's characters. He was a story-teller extraordinaire who was known during World War II while he was serving in the Army here. Those who remember him describe him as resembling Major Hoople, of the comic strip Major Hoople's Boarding House. He liked a drop of liquor and would, at the drop of a hat (or glass of beer, anyway) recount wonderful tales of his personal adventures.

Finnegan seemed to have been there whenever a major historical event took place, from the storming of the Bastille during the French Revolution in 1789 to the building of Cabot Tower in 1897. His story-telling was so captivating that he would hold his audience hanging on his every word, all the while making sure that his glass was filled. And he knew exactly when to start his story and what topic to choose for best effect, whether it was "I remember the year of the small potatoes" for a group of farmers, or his adventures fighting in the Spanish Civil War when someone in a pub happened to mention Spain.

The Poor House

One day on the Trivia Show we got into a discussion about a place that lived in St. John's infamy for many years: The Poor House.

It generated so much interest that even after the show was over people were calling me in the office to tell me their memories of the place, not as residents, but as people who had seen it and walked by it every day. The Poor House got its start after the St. John's fire of 1846. Sheds were erected to house the homeless victims of the fire and these were used until 1861. In 1860 a Government Act established a "poor asylum" for destitute persons who had no family or friends to support them, and who were incapable, "from extreme age, or physical infirmity", of looking after themselves. The people who had been living in the temporary shacks on the Parade grounds were moved en masse into the new facility on Sudbury Street (still known as "Poor House Lane" to some of the city's older residents). The Colony's Board of Works administered the asylum and admitted people on receipt of a certificate from a commissioner.

But once inside, people lost all their rights. Doors and gates were locked, they weren't permitted to leave the grounds without permission from the Keeper, there was no smoking, no drinking and the "inmates" were required to wear uniforms and to work for their keep. The overcrowded asylum received a lot of criticism by people who visited it. In 1907, a Grand Jury who examined the facility called it "the saddest place in Newfoundland". Eventually improvements were put into place. In 1931 it got a new name: The Home for the Aged and Infirm, and in 1949 some of the inmates were moved out to licensed boarding houses limiting the numbers at the home to 116. Then on August 2, 1965 the Poor House met its end. On that date the 120 men and women who were living there at the time were moved to Hoyles Home.

The Noonday Gun

As early as 1781 the Military Garrison in St. John's was using a cannon to signal time. According to the diary of Lt John Dun, the corporal of the guard would ring a bell at 9 AM, noon and 8 PM, and there was an evening gun. (In 1833 Sister Magdalene O'Shaugnessy, one of the founders of the Presentation Order of Nuns in Newfoundland, reported in a letter that St. John's had no town clock because the severity of the weather wouldn't enable it to be accurate, so, to mark the time, a gun was fired at certain times during the day. So perhaps the Noonday Gun has its origins in our "invigorating" climate.)

In 1852 the Royal Newfoundland Companies assumed responsibility for the firing of the gun. It was fired in the morning, in the evening and at noon. The morning and evening firings of the gun ended in 1869.

Until 1870, the gun was located at Queen's Battery on Signal Hill, but then it was moved near the summit of Signal Hill.

One of the best known incidents concerning the Noonday Gun happened in 1906, when a St. John's clergyman complained that the firing of the gun interfered with his sermons. The clergyman had enough influence to cause the Sunday firing to be stopped for several weeks. Maurice Devine immortalized the incident in his poem "Who Stopped the Gun?"

> "Now hasten forth, reporter man," the Editor did say
> "For some important news is out about the town
>   today;
> Go down to Skipper Eli Dawe and question him, my
>   son;
> He knows, I s'pose, who told Tom Rose to stop the
>   Sunday Gun."
> Then straight hied that reporter man to Skipper Eli
>   Dawe,
> And sought the information with considerable awe;
> "I cannot tell," the Skipper said, "but ask E.C.
>   Watson;
> He knows, I s'pose, who told Tom Rose to stop the
>   Sunday Gun."
> E.C. received the pencil-fiend with bland and kindly
>   smile,
> And said "I'll get the news you want in just a little
>   while;
> I'll inquire of H.C. Morris — he is out now for a run
> He knows, I s'pose, who told Tom Rose to stop the
>   Sunday Gun."
> 'Ere long the stalwart form of Mr. Morris hove in
>   sight;
> He said, "My dear reporter man, go call on Richard
>   White;

For information of this sort, good Richard takes the
    bun;
He knows, I s'pose, who told Tom Rose to stop the
    Sunday Gun.''
Good Richard, in his kindly way, received the
    wandering scribe,
And said he always had a liking for the tribe.
''But for such information, Captain English is the one;
He knows, I s'pose, who told Tom Rose to stop the
    Sunday Gun.''
The Captain calmly listened to the scribbler's tale of
    woe,
And said he always told the papers anything he'd
    know;
''Try Mr. Wheatley; he's the man who'll ask no
    better fun;
He knows, I s'pose, who told Tom Rose to stop the
    Sunday Gun.''
To Mr. Wheatley's private den the wanderer led the
    way;
But the lights were out, and doors were locked, it was
    the close of day;
But round the vaulted corridor an echoing did run;
''Who knows, I s'pose, who told Tom Rose to stop
    the Sunday Gun.''
The brave policeman on his beat was shocked at
    dawn of day
To find the body of a man, prone, lifeless, by the way;
The spirit of the puzzled scribe had flown beyond the
    sun;
And now knows, I s'pose, who told Tom Rose to stop
    the Sunday Gun.

(The various people mentioned in the poem were all
well-known public officials of the day. Eli Dawe was Minister
of Marine and Fisheries, whose department presumably had
some authority over the gun; E.C. Watson was superintendent

of fisheries, Captain English the Harbour Master and Richard White the superintendent of lighthouses).

The public raised such a ruckus over the silencing of the gun that it was reinstated after being out of commission for several weeks.

The gun was also stopped for a while in 1931 as an economy move by the government of Sir Richard Squires. On March 15, 1949 again it was silenced when it was found that it wasn't possible to find any more ammunition for it. This, tied with the Canadian Department of Transport's assuming responsibility for Cabot Tower, saw the Noonday Gun stopped until January 1, 1959. On that day the ceremony was revived, and it has continued ever since.

Over the years, several guns have served as the Noonday Gun. In 1870 it was a 12-pounder. By 1888 a 32-pounder was in use. In the early 1900s it was a muzzle-loading field gun from the Boer War, then in 1930, a 3-pounder Hotchkiss gun from the HMS *Briton*. A World War II 6-pounder anti-tank gun served for most of the 1960s.

In July 1994, a new 32-pounder became the latest Noonday Gun.

The Van Campers

This was one of those musical groups that I learned about purely by accident, when it popped up one day in a conversation I was having with Philip Hiscock of the MUN Folklore department. Philip had been doing some research on "The Barrelman" and had come across this group of performers and he wanted to know more about them. I mentioned it on the Trivia Show and was given a couple of leads which I passed on to Philip and he set to some further digging. Here's what he found:

During 1939 there was a series of concerts by a group known as the Van Campers. Joe Smallwood, as The Barrelman, had used the group on radio and they were popular enough that it was decided to do a series of shows at Pitt's

Memorial Hall in St. John's. (The group got its name from Van Camp's tinned beans, a product sold by Smallwood's sponsor, F. M. O'Leary.)

The members of the Van Campers were Bob MacLeod, VONF's studio musician, along with six other local musicians: Bill Moran ("he didn't play the accordion, he made it talk", said a friend of his 55 years later); drummer Bill Parrell; fiddle player Jack Tricco; xylophonist Jack Cronin; and singers Ray Elliott and Ray Lane.

All the musicians were experienced performers and many were members of an informal group of musicians who worked out of the Portugal Cove Road area. During the time that the group was performing, Smallwood published a series of "Barrelman Song Sheets", which contained about a dozen songs each. Several different series were published, including a Newfoundland series, and ones of English, Scottish and Irish songs. Unfortunately, Smallwood's interests didn't run too long in the direction of promoting Newfoundland music, and he soon forgot the Van Campers, who disbanded.

Ray Lane joined the services and went overseas. He died in England in 1940. Bill Moran joined the Newfoundland Foresters and went to Scotland during the War. He never returned to Newfoundland, living for a time after the War in England and in Bermuda. The others continued playing formally and informally in St. John's after the War.

Newfoundland's Bing Crosby

Another bit of trivia that Philip Hiscock found in his research of "The Barrelman":

In the *Daily News* of April 14, 1938 a story appeared which said that a "Galaxy of Radio Stars will appear at Radio Ball". One of the performers mentioned in the story is Donald Jamieson, whom the paper referred to as "Newfoundland's own Bing Crosby". Apparently the show was a great success and Don was mentioned again in the story that reported on it on April 25.

Then on May 13, 1938, again in the *Daily News*, there is an ad for the Queen Theatre which mentions Don Jamieson once again with the comment that his "voice will win its way into your heart". Oh, to have a recording of some of those performances!

The Confederation Building

According to some sources the height of the Confederation Building in St. John's is 454 feet, which would mean that the average ceiling height there would be over 30 feet! When the subject came up on the Trivia Show one day the figure didn't sound right to me so I decided to call the Works department at Confederation Building and set the record straight. The Confederation Building is 454 feet *above sea level*. The actual height of the building itself is 167 feet from the top of the front steps, and 217 feet from the boiler room in the back parking lot. Presumably, this measurement includes the cupola at the top of the Building, which was known to a generation of young Townies as "Joey's Office".

Gander's R.A.F. Side Buildings

What was unique about the names of the buildings on the R.A.F. Side in Gander during the 1940s and 1950s? They were named after planets. The two hotels for passengers using the airport were Saturn and Jupiter. The apartment buildings housing most families of people working at the airport were called Mars. The barracks for single personnel were known as Mercury, and one building housing three apartments for Eastern Provincial Airways personnel in the early and mid-1950s was called Venus. (I lived in Venus from 1953 to 1956). For some reason there were no buildings named after Earth, Neptune or Pluto. And I can certainly understand why "Uranus" was not chosen as a name for one of the dwellings.

The Lapland Reindeer Experiment

Reindeer may be associated with Santa Claus for most of us, and that image of eight reindeer (nine, if you include Rudolph) pulling Santa's sleigh through the air isn't far off the mark: the reindeer is considered to be quite a good work animal. Reindeer have been domesticated in northern Scandinavia and are considered much better than dogs for working because they can handle bigger loads, and travel farther in a shorter amount of time. They also can provide meat, milk, cheese, and leather which can be used for clothing.

In 1891, Dr. Sheldon Jackson imported a number of the creatures to Alaska to see how they would adapt to the area. He saw the animal as a possible saviour for the poverty stricken and half-starved natives in the area. Washington balked at what they considered a half-baked scheme. So Jackson lectured around the United States and finally raised about $5000 to try out his plan. He brought in a small herd of reindeer from Siberia, along with Siberian herders. The experiment was a resounding success.

In 1907 Dr. Wilfred Grenfell, recognizing that climatically Labrador was very similar to Alaska, and that Labrador natives could also benefit from the same sort of scheme, set out to duplicate Dr. Jackson's success.

Dr. Grenfell raised about $15,000 dollars. In September 1907 an official of Dr. Grenfell's Royal Deep Sea Mission bargained with the Norwegian government for a herd of 300 reindeer, along with three Lapp families and a supply of Lapland moss to feed the animals. The experiment was on.

On December 30 the Norwegian vessel *Anito* left Altenfjord on the coast of Lapland, headed for Newfoundland. She arrived 21 days later. The Newfoundland coast was icebound and the only way to get the cargo ashore was to put it on slob ice in Cremaillere Bay and use boats and dog teams to get it to shore. The reindeer were then put over the side. They took off in all directions, some of them heading for the open sea. But they were rounded up and, when the tally was finally taken, all were accounted for.

The Anglo-Newfoundland Development Company had bargained for 50 of the reindeer. They wanted them for hauling pulpwood and supplies during the winter. These animals were destined for Millertown.

Hugh Cole, Mattie Mitchell (the famous Micmac guide and prospector) and Tom Greening (who was the woods foreman for the A.N.D. Company) set out with the 50 reindeer and the Lapp herders for Millertown on March 3, 1908. The winter of 1908 turned out to be one of the worst winters on record in northern Newfoundland, but the group managed to travel on average about 13 miles a day. On April 30 they arrived at their destination. Only two animals had been lost. One had actually travelled all the way but had an injured leg and had to be shot.

Over the next few months the does gave birth to 25 fawns and it looked like the experiment would work out well. But then it was discovered that the area around Millertown did not produce enough moss to feed the herd, so it was decided to send the animals back to St. Anthony. This time though, they travelled by boat.

Back in St. Anthony, the other 250 animals were also proving to be a hardy lot, and the experiment was being touted as a success.

Two years after it began, Dr. Grenfell was still optimistic that it would be a success and that sending the reindeer to Labrador would be a great boon to the natives there. But, before long, problems started to arise. The Lapps were a discontented lot and wanted to return home. Then, the reindeer were attacked by dogs and killed by poachers. Grenfell implored authorities to help, but to no avail. They seemed to consider a vote more important than the welfare of the animals. Then the War intervened and with food shortages and attention being focused elsewhere, the size of the herd shrunk from the 1500 it had grown to, down to 230.

When Grenfell returned from France (where he'd served with the Harvard Surgical Unit) he realized it was futile to continue the project, so he offered what was left of the herd to the Canadian Government, who accepted. Ironically, just as the deal was the signed the Newfoundland government came through with some of the assistance that Grenfell had requested before. One hundred twenty-five of the surviving animals were sent to Anticosti Island, where they eventually died off.

However, it may be that some of the caribou herd of the Great Northern Peninsula are descendants of Dr. Grenfell's reindeer! Biologists consider reindeer to be the same species as Newfoundland caribou, while there are accounts that the reindeer and local caribou ranged together during mating season. Further, the lungworm that infests many Newfoundland caribou is considered to be of European origin, and some scientists believe that the parasite was brought here by the Lapp reindeer.

The Building of Goose Bay Airport

In June 1987, *Them Days* magazine (a Newfoundland and Labrador treasure, in my opinion) ran a special issue devoted to the history of Goose Bay. Anyone with an interest in the area should read it. Here are a few pieces of trivia that came from that issue:

The site for Goose Bay Airport was recommended by F.T. Jenkins, a Canadian forestry engineer. He'd been in the area and was consulted in the winter of 1940-41 about the best place to put an airfield in Labrador. His recommendations were the North West River open scrub plain, or The Backway, which was 120 miles east (near Rigolet). Because Jenkins had been doing a timber survey and hadn't been looking specifically at sites for an airfield, the RCAF called in a surveyor, Eric (Jack) Fry, to determine which would be better.

On June 16, 1941 Fry arrived in North West River. After some searching he determined that the best location would be an area known as "Robert's Berry Bank" (locally, I have heard the area described as "Uncle Bob's Berry Patch"). On June 20 he wrote a dispatch informing his superiors of his find and changed the name of the site to the "Hamilton River Site".

After surveying the area for many days he re-named it again: "The Goose Bay Site", after the nearby Goose River.

Unlike Doug Fraser who found the location for Gander airport from an airplane, Jack Fry had no idea what the Labrador site looked like from the air until July 15 when he finally got to fly over the area in a Catalina flying boat.

The contract to build the airport was awarded to McNamara Construction in September 1941. Within 10 days three men had gone into the area and, after recruiting local fishermen and trappers to help, they began work. Within five months the airport was in operation. It was, at the time, one of the largest airports in the world. The project had cost around $20,000,000.

The first aircraft to land there was a ski-equipped twin-engine plane owned by Quebec Airways which landed on December 3, 1941. The first military aircraft landed on December 9.

The first RCAF detachment commander at Goose Bay was Squadron leader W.J. McFarlane. The airport officially became RCAF station Goose Bay on April 1, 1942.

On December 10, 1942, three days after Pearl Harbour, a C-39 of the United States Air Force began moving personnel and supplies into Goose Bay.

Tidbits

The famous Newfoundland folk song "The Ryans and the Pittmans" was written by Newfoundland historian and deputy minister of His Majesty's Customs, Henry W. LeMessurier. Sung to the tune of the well-known sea-chantey "Spanish Ladies", the song's lyrics describe several communities on the west side of Placentia Bay, which LeMessurier had represented as MHA for Burin in the 1880s.

In my first book I listed the vessels of the Alphabet Fleet. This time we have the "Splinter Fleet": a fleet of 10 ships built for the Newfoundland Department of Natural Resources during the mid-1940s. They were all built at Clarenville from the same plans and each was named for a Newfoundland community. They were the *Bonne Bay*, *Burin*, *Clarenville*,

Codroy, Exploits, Ferryland, Glenwood, Placentia, Trepassey and *Twillingate.*

Less well-known are the four ships produced at Marystown by the Department of Natural Resources during its first attempt to start a shipyard. Between 1939, when the Marystown program was begun, and 1941, when the yard was destroyed in a fire, four ships were built and named after islands in Placentia Bay: the *Jude, Marticot, Merasheen* and *Oderin.* All four were pressed into wartime service as minesweepers.

The M.V. *Kipawo* was a well-known Newfoundland vessel. Unlike so many other Newfoundland ships which ended up in a scrap heap somewhere, the *Kipawo* found a new life. In Parrsboro, Nova Scotia, the *Kipawo* is home to the Ship's Company troupe as a floating theatre.

One of Newfoundland's more prolific trees, the trembling aspen, is said to have been called "woman's tongue" by the Indians because of the constant fluttering of its leaves.

Being a fan of Western movies from my childhood, I'd heard the term "redskin" used to describe Indians long before I'd ever heard that there had been Indians in Newfoundland. According to many sources, the term "redskin" was first applied to the Beothuk of Newfoundland — who were, after all, the first North American Indians to have contact with Europeans. The Beothuk used to cover their bodies with red ochre — thought by some anthropologists either to have religious significance or to be an insect repellent! The term was later applied to North American Indians in general.

When Mount Pearl became a city there was a standing joke (mostly among Townies) that it was the only city in the world without an elevator. I was quick to point out this wasn't true. There was in fact at least one elevator at the time — in the Commonwealth Medical Clinic Building. Mount Pearl has really blossomed since achieving its charter and now there are lots of elevators. And you can even buy a suit of clothes there

— which was another reason some people said Mount Pearl wasn't a real city.

In 1875 the Church of England Girl's school in St. John's (the fore-runner to Bishop Spencer College) got a new principal named Clara Butler. Ms. Butler was from Quebec. It's said that she used to teach her classes with a pet monkey perched on her shoulder.

In *Newfoundland and Labrador Trivia* I listed the National Historic Sites in the Province. There are a couple to add, so here's the complete list, including the updates. There are eight National Historic Sites in Newfoundland and Labrador: Signal Hill National Historic Site in St. John's; Cape Spear National Historic Site; Castle Hill National Historic Site at Jerseyside, Placentia Bay; Port au Choix National Historic Site; L'Anse aux Meadows National Historic Site; Red Bay National Historic Site; and two new sites which are (as of this writing) in development and not open to the public yet. These two are Hawthorne Cottage National Historic Site at Brigus, and the Ryan Premises National Historic Site at Bonavista.

In addition to these "sites" there are also a number of locations around the Province which have been noted by Parks Canada to be of significant historic interest and which have been marked with plaques. There are over 50 of these.

Religion

This chapter could easily fill a book itself. However, rather than concentrating on the whys and wherefores of religion in Newfoundland and Labrador or doing a sociological study (something for which I am hardly qualified), I'll stick to the trivia and milestones, concentrating on the Church of England, Roman Catholic, Methodist (United Church), Salvation Army and Pentecostal churches.

Church of England

The Church of England was the first officially established church in Newfoundland. When Sir Humphrey Gilbert took possession of Newfoundland for the Queen of England in 1583, one of the regulations he outlined was that the practising of religion would be done according to the Church of England.

The first clergyman was Rev. Erasmus Stourton, who arrived with John Guy around 1610.

The first clergyman to receive the sanction of the Society for the Propagation of the Gospel was John Jackson, who arrived with his family in 1701. (More about Rev. Jackson later in the chapter).

The first Bishop of the Church of England to set foot in Newfoundland was Bishop Charles Inglis, of the diocese of Nova Scotia and Newfoundland, in 1787. Both Bishop's Falls, in central Newfoundland, and the community of Bishop's Cove, Conception Bay, were named in his honour.

In 1839 Rev. Aubrey Spencer was consecrated as the first Bishop of the Diocese of Newfoundland and Bermuda. (Guess which part of the diocese that he preferred for his vacations!)

In 1976 the Diocese of Newfoundland was restructured into three dioceses: Eastern Newfoundland and Labrador, Western Newfoundland and Central Newfoundland.

Roman Catholic

Although the origins of the Roman Catholic Church in Newfoundland are the subject of debate ranging from St. Brendan to the Vikings to John Cabot, it is documented that Jacques Cartier had chaplains with him when he explored the Gulf of St. Lawrence, and when Lord Baltimore arrived in the 1620s he was accompanied by three Jesuit Priests who celebrated mass regularly. But it wasn't until 1784 that the church in Newfoundland received official recognition from Rome.

The first Bishop of the Roman Catholic Church in Newfoundland was James Louis O'Donel, who was consecrated in 1796.

Life wasn't easy for the first practitioners of Roman Catholicism in Newfoundland. There are stories of priests being beaten and persecuted; and people who allowed Mass to be celebrated in their homes were fined, imprisoned, flogged or had their houses torn down or burned.

Sister Mary Bernard Kirwan of Ireland was the Mother Superior of the first order of Presentation Nuns to serve in Newfoundland — the Southern Shore community of Port Kirwan was named after her.

The first Mother Superior and founder of Our Lady of Mercy School in St. John's was Sister Mary Frances Creedon.

Methodist Church

The first minister of John Wesley's Methodist Church to come to Newfoundland was Rev. Laurence Coughlan who arrived in 1765 — sort of. Coughlan wasn't sent by Wesley, but by the Society for the Propagation of the Gospel in Foreign Parts, which had supported Church of England chaplains on our shores. Coughlan was a supporter of Wesley's efforts to reform the Church of England and corresponded with the founder of the Methodist Church concerning Newfoundland, but was at least nominally a clergyman of the Church of England.

In 1813 the Wesleyan Methodist Missionary Society was formed in England and in 1815 a district was organized in Newfoundland consisting of six ministers.

In 1859 three more missions were added to the list including Labrador.

The first Newfoundland conference of the Methodist Church of Canada was organized in 1874 with Rev. G.S. Milligan as President.

In 1925 the Methodist Church changed its named to United Church.

Presbyterian Church

The Presbyterian Church had Newfoundland origins with the Scots merchants who lived in St. John's. Although there were Presbyterians in Newfoundland prior to 1842, it wasn't until that year that the church was officially established here. On Christmas Eve, 1841 Rev. Donald Allan Fraser arrived with his son, after being invited to come here by some of the residents. The remaining members of his family arrived in the new year.

Work began almost immediately on the building of the Church (or Kirk) and St. Andrew's Church officially opened on December 3, 1843. For a time all went well, until the death of Rev. Fraser in 1845. Then the congregation was split on who was to succeed him. The result was the separation into two groups: The Free Church group and the Established Church group.

In 1870 Rev J.D. Paterson arrived and the church began to come back together, but there were still obstacles to the reunion. But in 1876 both churches burned to the ground. The catastrophe resulted in people coming back together as one congregation.

In 1925 discussions were underway to bring together the Methodist, Congregational and Presbyterian Churches in Canada. The result was that the three united to become the United Church of Canada. In Newfoundland, the subject of Church Union was discussed among the Presbyterians. It was eventually decided to keep a separate identity. (The small Newfoundland Congregationalist Church also decided to remain separate, but eventually some congregations did join the United Church, while in St. John's the Congregationalists joined forces with the Presbyterians).

Salvation Army

The Salvation Army was started by William Booth in England in 1865, and had spread to Newfoundland by 1886. Charles Dawson and his new bride, Emma Churchill, were early converts to the Salvation Army in Ontario. On their honeymoon they were visiting Emma's parents in Portugal Cove and they took the opportunity to hold meetings at Temperance Hall in St. John's.

The first attempt at holding a formal gathering in St. John's didn't go too well. Colonel Arthur Young and other officers of the Salvation Army arrived in Newfoundland in 1886 and held an open-air gathering on the Parade Ground. People were attracted from all over the city, not so much by an opportunity to receive the gospel, but to gawk at the newcomers and their uniforms. The crowd got out of hand and the police were called in, and the Salvation Army officers escaped with only minor injuries.

The group managed to find a hall on Springdale Street and held gatherings there. At their marches they had to be accompanied by members of the police to keep the peace.

But the Salvationists were undaunted and eventually, when the residents saw that the group only had the interests of the community at heart, they were left alone.

In 1994 Newfoundland remains one of the Salvation Army's strongholds: nearly one-third of the total Salvation Army membership in all of Canada lives in the Province, while the Army in central Canada is also dominated by ex-patriate Newfoundlanders. The General (or international head) of the Salvation Army in 1993-94, Bramwell Tillsley, was for many years an officer in Newfoundland. Mrs. General Tillsley is the former Maude Pitcher of Winterton, Trinity Bay.

Pentecostal Assemblies

The Pentecostal Church in Newfoundland got its start through the work of Alice Belle Garrigus. She was born in the United States in 1858 and drifted from place to place and from faith to faith until 1907, when she met a Pentecostal preacher named Frank Bartleman. It was then that she was converted to Pentecostalism.

In October 1908, she received "a message from God" telling her to go to Newfoundland. In 1910 she had another message which again told her that her mission was in Newfoundland. But her view of Newfoundland was of a place that was (in her words) "a frozen up country, no civilization, possibly inhabited by Esquimaux". Then she received a message from a retired couple named the Fowlers who said they had also received a message from God instructing them to accompany Alice to Newfoundland. They arrived in St. John's on December 1, 1910 and set about building their congregation. On Easter Sunday, 1911, they opened the doors of Bethesda Tabernacle to the public in downtown St. John's.

The Pentecostal Church in Newfoundland continued to build with Assemblies springing up all over Newfoundland and Labrador. In the 1930s the church had two boats which brought the gospel to some of the more isolated regions. The *Gospel Messenger* travelled along the Labrador Coast and the northern French Shore, while the *Good Tidings* sailed along the southern shore.

Moravian Church

The Moravian Church in Labrador got off to a very shaky start. In 1752 a Dutch pilot named Johann Christian Erhardt, who had been converted in 1741, arrived in Labrador. Erhardt wanted to bring the Gospel to natives of Hudson's Bay, but he was rejected by the Hudson's Bay Company, who refused to allow anyone preaching to natives in the vicinity of their factories. But Erhardt, along with four missionaries, got passage on an English vessel, the *Hope*, and set out for

Labrador. The ship reached the south-eastern coast in July 1752, where they were welcomed by the natives. A house was built with materials brought from England in a place the missionaries called Nisbet's Harbour (probably near Hopedale).

Some time after their arrival Erhardt set sail up the coast in the *Hope*. Two weeks later the ship arrived back at Nisbet's Harbour with a sad story. Erhardt, the ship's captain, and five sailors had landed up the coast with merchandise they hoped to trade with the natives. The mate and the rest of the crew remained on board the *Hope* and waited. Several days passed and there was no sign. Finally the mate gave orders to return the ship to Nisbet's Harbour. It was believed that Erhardt's party had been killed by the natives.

Now short of a crew, the mate asked the remaining missionaries to help him get the ship back to England. They did and so ended the first attempt to set up a mission in Labrador.

It wasn't until 1764 that the Moravians tried again to establish a mission in the area. In that year a Moravian carpenter named Jens Haven set out for Newfoundland with letters of introduction for the governor, Sir Hugh Palliser. Palliser encouraged Haven on his way and the missionary headed for Labrador. Upon his arrival he was welcomed by the Eskimos but shortly afterwards Haven returned to England. At the urging of a native woman named Mikak who was in England, Haven prepared a new expedition to Labrador. In the meantime, the English Privy Council had granted the Moravians 100 acres of land anywhere on the coast that they wanted to settle "for the purpose of evangelizing the heathen inhabitants".

Haven arrived back in Labrador in 1770 and after developing a friendly relationship with the natives, he and his companion, a Danish missionary named Christian Lorenz Drachart, returned to England and made arrangements for an even bigger mission to Labrador. In 1771, Haven, Drachart, and 13 others set out for Labrador. They set up a mission station at a place 80 miles north of Hopedale, a place they called Nain. And so began the first successful Moravian church in Labrador.

The Rev. John Jackson & Company

And finally, a story that has romance, intrigue, action, sex — all the ingredients to make a successful movie or novel. And it's all true.

Anyone who ever tells you that Newfoundland history is boring obviously hasn't done much reading in it.

If I may get on my soap box for a moment, in my humble opinion, one area in which education fails in this Province is the way in which history was taught. When I was going to school I HATED history. I make no bones about it. I hated it with a passion. It was dull, it was boring, a collage of dates and facts which meant nothing to me it all. I couldn't care less. "But it tells us where we came from and how we've evolved", we were told. Oh Yeah? Well, if that's the case, we were dull, dull, dull.

It was only when I saw history reflected in the stories of real people that it made any sense to me. When I read about Peter Easton or Mary March or D'Iberville this mess of facts got through. We do the same thing in journalism.... It's fine to say AIDS kills thousands of people. Sure it means something, but it means a lot more when we hear the story of one or two people who've been afflicted with the disease. Remember the effect the story of Ray Condon in Labrador had on us all? It did more to show us the impact of this disease than all the statistics you could muster up. And so it is with history. For example: in the early 18th Century, residents of St. John's along with the local clergyman were at loggerheads with the military and a number of incidents resulted which caused the British powers to institute some changes. YAWN.

But, here is a story which much better reflects the era because it puts names on the people who lived through those times, and gives us a better sense of what life was like then:

In *Newfoundland and Labrador Trivia* I made some brief reference to the work of the Rev. John Jackson, the first Church of England clergyman to be supported in his work in Newfoundland by the Society for the Propagation of the Gospel. Then I started finding these little bits and pieces of information about Rev. Jackson and those around him which made for what I consider to be one of the most fascinating stories I've ever read about the early years in our Country's history. This is a story that deserves to get some attention by motion picture producers. Really, it has all the elements to make a hit movie. The main players are Rev. John Jackson, his wife, Captain Thomas Lloyd of the Independent Companies and his replacement Lieutenant John Moody.

In 1699 residents of St. John's felt it was high time to have a resident priest, so they sent off a request to the Bishop of London. Rev. John Jackson (who, it is believed, had visited the island as a naval chaplain in 1697) got the job and was sent to Newfoundland along with his family. He arrived on July 12, 1701. In no time at all Jackson and the commander of the garrison at St. John's were at odds. At the time the military ruled supreme in St. John's. What they said was the law. Jackson felt that the officers of the fort were oppressing both the ordinary soldiers and the settlers.

He complained to the officers through official channels, but that only riled them up more. So Jackson wrote the Bishop of London complaining about his treatment by Captain Powell and Lieutenant Francis of the Independent Companies. Instructions came back to the commanders that the clergyman was not to be ill-treated.

But it was just starting. The battle between Jackson and the military officials hit its peak with the arrival of Thomas Lloyd as commanding officer of the Independent Companies. Jackson complained about Lloyd's brutality and of the way that Lloyd would swindle the settlers for his own profit. In one letter to the Commissioners of Trade and Plantations in London,

Jackson accused Lloyd of everything from cruelty to theft to adultery.

According to Jackson, on the Sabbath Lloyd would parade around the harbour with his fiddle in an attempt to divert people away from church. Then the rest of the day Lloyd and his companions would engage in "dancing and rioting with their whores". Given the choice of partaking in divine services or a sex orgy, some of the residents were opting for the latter. Jackson also said that one of Lloyd's lady friends was a notorious thief and prostitute, who had been given such power by her lover that any soldier who disobeyed her could find himself being whipped.

The message finally got through and Lloyd was eventually called back to London. His successor was Lieutenant John Moody. Moody and the Rev. Mr. Jackson hit it off beautifully. Suddenly all was well again.

But there was another side to the story. According to Lloyd and some others, Jackson was the one who was the disruptive influence in the Colony. In the winter of 1704-05, while Lloyd, Captain Michael Richards (Lloyd's predecessor) and Captain Timothy Bridges were in London they reported to the Board of Trade. The board in turn reported to the Bishop of London that the "irregular proceedings [in Newfoundland] have been in great measure occasioned by the violent temper and scandalous life of Mr. Jackson the minister." They accused Jackson of heavy drinking. But the incident which probably got Jackson in the deepest trouble involved his wife, who was one strict lady, and their servant girl. One day after the girl had made the family beds Mrs. Jackson took exception to the way it had been done and proceeded to verbally abuse the servant. The girl, instead of standing there and taking the haranguing, proceeded to give Mrs. Jackson as good as m'lady was dishing out. This upset the minister's wife no end, and she threw the girl out. The good reverend, upon learning of the incident, told the story to his buddy John Moody. Moody took the girl into the fort, disciplined her and threw her out into the cold.

Residents were ordered that they were not to take the young girl into their homes. Even though they'd been warned, some people took pity on her and brought her in for a warm. But it was too late. The young girl died shortly after.

When Jackson's old enemy, Thomas Lloyd, learned the story, he used it as part of his evidence against the clergyman.

Another incident involving Rev. Jackson and his wife is recounted by Bampfylde Moore-Carew, the man known as the King of the Beggars, in his autobiography. (The story of Moore-Carew is mentioned elsewhere in this book). Moore-Carew was back in England masquerading as Aaron Cock, a St. John's planter. He wanted to get some provisions and was being questioned by a number of people who wanted to verify his identity. These were people who had been to Newfoundland and knew some of the residents. One of the stories they asked him about concerned an event which happened at the home of Aaron Cock's father one evening. Moore-Carew knew it well. He related how the incident occurred at a social gathering with Rev. Jackson, Governor John Collins and several of the ladies from the town. They were all having a few drinks. At some point during the evening, Governor Collins, who was unmarried, said that he felt there wasn't an honest woman in all of Newfoundland. The party-goers were a little taken aback by the comment. Rev Jackson asked "What about my wife?". Collins said "The same as all other women. They're all whores." Mrs. Jackson and a group of the ladies (I use the term lightly) pounced on Collins, pinning him to the floor. They ripped his clothes, and lashed out at his face with their fingernails, disfiguring him. Mrs. Jackson, meanwhile, grabbed a knife and slashed the ham-string of Collins' leg. It left him a cripple for the rest of his life.

In November 1705, Jackson and his family left Newfoundland on board the *Falkland* to return to London. In the convoy of ships there was also a vessel (the *Looe*) carrying Moody and Bridges. On the way the ships hit a violent storm and, although there was no loss of life, the Jackson family lost most of their possessions. When they arrived in England Jackson asked the Board of Trade that he be excused from immediate attendance at a hearing into his conduct in Newfoundland because he was feeling the effects of the shipwreck. They agreed to his request. Eventually the board began to feel pity for Rev. Jackson and in 1706 wrote the Bishop of London a letter in which they said "we commend this unfortunate man to your custody".

Jackson moved to Dursley in Gloucestershire in 1709 and became curate there. In 1710 he became rector of Uley. Rev John Jackson died in 1717.

So if anyone ever says we have a dull and boring past, tell them to read the story of the Rev. Jackson, or Dobbin the Diver, or the Society of Masterless Men. The adventures and intrigue are as good as you'll find anywhere.

Art Rockwood was born in 1946 at Whitbourne (well, actually, it was at Markland Cottage Hospital) and spent most of his early life in Gander, living in Venus from 1953 to 1956. It was in Gander that his interest in trivial matters began. Well inland from the distractions of the sea, the airport town was probably one of the most cosmopolitan places in Newfoundland at the time. Gander was also well provided with North American cultural influences due to the numbers of servicemen stationed there. Art could be found lying on the floor in front of the TV or with his ear glued to the radio, while other boys were off playing hockey or baseball. Anything and everything about music, television shows, movies and the people who worked in these businesses was obviously of paramount importance. Although this unfortunately left very little brainpower to spare for his schoolwork, he did graduate from Gander Academy in 1963, then worked for a year before going on to Memorial University.

He soon became interested in a career in radio broadcasting, and began working with CHCM in Marystown in 1966. He later joined the CBC, working with CBG in Gander from 1968 to 1979 and then moving to St. John's. In 1981 he began the "Trivia Show" on CBC radio, which has since become a popular regular feature of the program "Radio Noon". His first book, *Art Rockwood's Newfoundland and Labrador Trivia*, was published in 1993.